Best wishes to F
— lovely to m

Midge Frayne
Fairyhill
June 2005

TO

My Late Friend

DIANE BUTTON

A
GOWER STRIPPER

By

Midge Frayne

GOWER

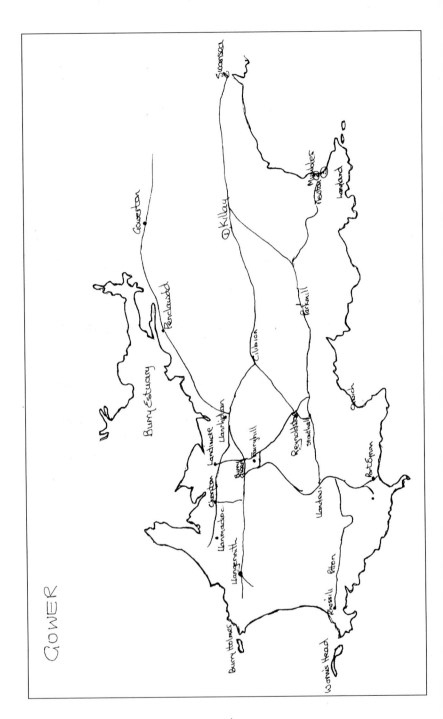

Foreword

'FAIRYHILL' – a magical name for a magical place.

Set in the heart of the Gower Peninsula and hidden from the world behind its high gates, shuttered windows and overgrown parklands. Thirty-five years of vandalism by neglect had strangled the once magnificent gardens and left the house in a state of near collapse and complete loss of dignity.

The thought of actually owning this part of history and being allowed to restore it excited John and me so much that it dominated our thoughts for most of the time. And if we could have seen into the future, it was to engulf us totally and take us over body and soul for the next ten years.

Chapter One

"You've gone too far this time". My mother's words came at me protestingly. "Are you completely crazy? How can you leave a wonderful home like Burry Cottage for that disaster?" My mother thought John and I totally mad to take on Fairyhill. This, from a woman who had tackled anything in her time but now, I suppose, in her declining years, the thought of all that work was too much for her to contemplate.

She had been a strong, powerful lady who was not afraid to knock down a wall or indeed, build one. It's her I have to thank (or otherwise) for my determination to 'have a go' and I have the same satisfaction from renovating and decorating houses that she had.

My first house was brand new and I hated it. I had married for the first time in 1963 at the age of twenty-five. Most young couples seemed to be buying new houses at that time. It was on a new estate in Killay, on the outskirts of Swansea.

I did all I could to make it different from the hundreds of others but I just had to accept it for what it was – soulless.

We stayed there for only two years before buying a two-bedroomed cottage in Mumbles. Jim, my first husband, didn't really want to move. He was quite happy in Killay in the modern house. Maybe another reason was the fact that the cottage was next door to Jo, my sister.

It had, in fact, been converted from the rear part of a larger house but very well done with some original features – stone fireplace, oak beams in the kitchen and an open plan wooden stairs. Unfortunately, the beams and staircase had been varnished and the fireplace painted. It took me a long time to strip these, especially the stonework, but I'm very determined and I did a bit at a time telling myself that it would be well worth the effort. My mother would come occasionally to give me a hand.

The bathroom had a wonderful iron bath – very deep and long. The only snag was the colour – eau-de-Nil. This colour was also on the tiles together with a nasty blue and the whole thing was made much worse by the cream gloss paint on all the walls and ceiling. Very Corporation!

I spent many lunchtimes searching for the right wallpaper and eventually I found it. William Morris type – a very bold, all-over pattern containing the same green and blue as the tiles and bath. It was very dramatic and I put it above the tiles, on the ceiling and also on the bath panel. It detracted wonderfully from the tiles.

All this work is very insignificant really and my point in mentioning it is not for admiration but merely as an object in human behaviour.

A while after selling this cottage, the new owners insisted that I visit them so they could show me their improvements. Yes, you've guessed – they had varnished the beams and stairs, painted the stone fireplace and stripped the wallpaper from the bathroom and painted it – cream gloss!

I was upset and then cross, but I soon saw the funny side and couldn't wait to relate the story, which I have done on numerous occasions.

Jim and I had only lived in Mumbles a short while when we split up. I returned home from work one day and my sister told me he had gone. That would have been 1967 and I never set eyes on him again. I have often thought that I would like to meet up with him to see what happened to his life after he left and if he has been as happy as I. It all seems like another lifetime.

Anyway, I was now left on my own. My mother assumed I would return home to live with her but I was determined to keep my independence and manage on my own.

I stayed on in my little cottage for a couple more years, struggling with various repairs. It was quite damp on one outside wall and I managed to find a builder who did a good job at a reasonable price. His name was Elwyn and he was to play quite a part in the next few years.

My sister and I visited our local pub, the Newton Inn, quite a lot. This was run by Iori and Millie Evans at that time. Millie had made a point, on my marriage break up, of telling me I was always welcome and not to be shy about coming in any time. She would always be there to chat to. This was in the days when women didn't go to pubs on their own as they do now. The Newton was quite an institution in those days and, indeed, is still very popular. For me, it was a sanity saver and I was very grateful.

It was in the Newton that I first met John. It certainly wasn't love at first sight but he made me laugh and we seemed to be on the same wave length. We were very comfortable together.

He had parted from his wife two years previously after a twelve-year marriage and had a son, Simon who was then five years old and whom he took out every Sunday afternoon.

He was running the shoe business that his father had started fifty years previously. His father had been rather a dictator and when the shop was bombed during the Blitz on Swansea, had gone to Cowbridge where John, at the age of thirteen was still in boarding school, and physically removed him from the classroom. He had re-opened the shop in the front room of their house in St. James' Crescent and John sold his first pair of shoes that afternoon.

Poor John, it was always his ambition to travel but he was to be in that shop for the next forty two years

He specialised in fitting feet of all widths from the narrowest to the widest – small and large. I have very narrow feet and he had been fitting them since I was a little girl. He didn't remember me but recognised my feet!

He was, and still is, the most enthusiastic person I have ever met and throws himself totally into whatever interests him. He lived for the business and truly believed that the customer was always right. Nothing was too much trouble and his aim was to please. He was acknowledged as the leading shoe fitter in the British Isles and indeed, designed many himself. Shoes from Fraynes were sent all over the world.

At this time he had one shop in the Kingsway which is in the centre of Swansea and another in Neath, about ten miles away. A few years later he was to sell the Neath shop and open a second one also in Swansea city centre, selling men's and ladies' fashions in addition to shoes.

When we first met, John was living with one of his sisters in Sketty but soon afterwards he bought a one-bedroom flat in Langland. This was only about a mile from me so he was always popping in.

We spent more and more time together. Sunday and Wednesday nights were unmissable. We travelled to Pontardulais – about fifteen miles away where the male voice choir practised. As soon as the practice was over a large group would meet at the Fountain Inn and, when all whistles were wet enough, the singing would start.

The sound was all-engulfing. To hear them in concert was wonderful but to be totally surrounded was an emotional experience hard to describe. Their songs are many and varied: Welsh hymns, popular songs, opera. My visit was mainly hymns, with Old McDonald's Farm thrown in. Then, to totally annihilate me emotionally – 'Martyrs of the Arena'. This is a real gut-buster that left my stomach wobbling and my neck hairs rigid.

A night at the Fountain could not be missed. John had been going there since the choir had been formed, seven years previously. He had taken dozens of people and tended to judge them by their reactions. Some were totally unmoved. I think I had passed the test.

We got married two years after meeting in February 1972. Just us and two friends as witnesses. We went to Mallorca for ten days honeymoon – taking sixteen of the Pontardulais boys with us. People found this hard to believe but we loved them and didn't think it strange. We had a wonderful time but that would make another book.

When we returned from our honeymoon (it took everyone ten days to recover) we were surprised to see a 'For Sale' sign on the next door property, number 4 Overland Road. This was a house that had always fascinated me. Old and neglected with an overgrown driveway leading up to it. Double fronted and rambling with half an acre of 'garden'.

I couldn't wait to see inside and soon arranged to pick up the key. We had a good poke around and it really was in an awful state – and smelly. It was a sturdy house with a very large sitting room on one side and two smaller rooms on the other. A long passage led through to the kitchen, scullery, three pantries and a wonderful back stairs. It hadn't been touched for decades but appeared quite strong structurally. There were nine rooms upstairs including two attic rooms.

John had never seen this side of me. I rushed from room to room mentally planning it all. I loved it. He kept muttering how unbelievably awful it was and that nothing could make it livable. We stood on the front lawn and I remember saying, "John, I promise that if you buy it, I can make it into something really worth having." He must have had blind faith in me, and he agreed. Since then he has always supported me when I wanted to do something.

There was quite a lot of interest in the house and it eventually went to auction. We had decided on the price we would go to and if it went higher, we would buy a boat instead! How events can change one's life.

Needless to say, we got it at the pre-agreed price and decided to make plans. We contacted Elwyn straight away and he came for a good look and to give us a rough estimate for the roof and various other skilled jobs.

It took a while to sell my cottage but we could get started on number 4. Being only next door it was very convenient. Although both properties had long driveways, we could just pop through the hedge.

I was so happy and totally fulfilled. I continued with my part-time job. This was in a solicitors' practice, Beor Wilson and Lloyd, where I had worked full time for the last ten years. I had tried to finish altogether but had been persuaded to stay on, mornings only. All that meant was the same amount of work in half the time! I have always enjoyed a challenge so took it in my stride. I couldn't wait until one o'clock every day when I rushed home to continue my scraping, painting and papering and the excitement of moving on to the next room. Elwyn was turning up every day and we were making good progress.

This was where I had my first arch. It had always been an ambition to have one and Elwyn said he could do it easily. He knocked down part of the wall between the two smallish rooms on the left of the front door and made a big dining room with the arch in the middle. It looked wonderful and I was thrilled.

Needless to say, the people who eventually bought the house from us, four years later, separated these rooms again by blocking up my lovely arch with glass doors.

We had to buy quite a lot of furniture as I didn't have much and John had sold his modern furniture with the flat. The only thing he had from his previous marriage was a wonderful carved oak sideboard that he had bought in an auction sale. His ex-wife hated it and when he left he was told to "take that monstrosity with you." We have called it the 'monstrosity' ever since.

We were lucky to find a superb Welsh dresser. Well, John was the one who found it – in a tiny antique shop in Neath. He happened to be in the shop when it was carried in, complete with fourteen copper lustre jugs. He telephoned me to say that he had found a dresser and, like a typical woman I said, "Wait until I see it". At this time I was still not sure of his taste and, I suppose, if I'm honest, I thought I knew best. "Too late," he said. "I've already bought it." Well, of course, it was beautiful and that was the first and last time I ever questioned his judgment.

The first thing John did when we moved in was to buy some chickens. Unheard of in this area but we had a big enough garden and at the rear of the property was a huge field so our chickens just popped through the hedge and scratched around happily. We did well for eggs and were able to supply the shop staff with some of the surplus. We slipped up once when we failed to spot the wild garlic growing in the field. We both love garlic but added to food – not included. Needless to say the eggs were inedible and we had to write them off until the garlic had finished.

Our only pets at this time were a dog and a cat. Pippin was a spaniel and really belonged to my sister, Jo. He was mostly with me when I lived in the cottage and we used to agree that we had half each. I had the half that ate and went to the Vet!

John wasn't very keen on cats but quite liked Jenkins, a tabby who was full of character. Unfortunately, poor Jenkins didn't live very long after having an accident so I quickly found two kittens before John had time to think.

Anyone who has had a kitten knows what time wasters they are, but two – what a disaster! We just sat and watched them for hours on end. We began by calling them Sugar and Spice but somehow this soon changed to Lil and Nellie after two of John's ancient aunts.

Elwyn was getting on well but gradually had stopped eating his packed lunch and had begun visiting the Victoria pub down the road. What we eventually came to understand was that he was alcoholic and had been 'dried out' more than once. He was very reasonable and only stayed at the pub for an hour and this didn't interfere with his work.

I remember one day he was putting up scaffolding on the side of the house to get to the chimney. He was getting near the top, which was extremely high and said he had to go for help before tackling the last bit. We assumed he was going for a mate but his 'help' was a few pints down the 'Vic'. On his return he all but ran up the scaffolding and threw the last piece into place!

It was at this time that John took over a new shop in Mumbles. He had always liked the idea of one in that area but there was never anything available. Not a person to be put off a project, he decided to go into every shop to ask if they wanted to sell. At the third attempt he succeeded in acquiring 'Turgoose' which was a lovely old-fashioned grocers.

He advertised the sale of all groceries 'half price to pensioners' and had a long queue on the appointed day. Not to miss out on any free publicity, he telephoned the TV newsline and a cameraman was there in no time. We appeared that evening on the local news.

I had often accompanied John when he was buying shoes and Val and I always bought the ladies' fashions and menswear with him. Val had started out as John's secretary but was now running the fashion department of the Portland Street shop.

I had never been involved in the retail side and had absolutely no wish to have any part in it. I knew what was going to happen as soon as he bought the Mumbles shop.

"Come into the shop Midge, you'd be great."

"No thank you, John, I would hate it."

"No you wouldn't, you'd be really good."

I could think of nothing worse. Working in a shop had never appealed to me – and a shoe shop – horrors! Although I had worked all my life, I had never been involved with the general public.

Well, John could never take no for an answer and before I knew it, I was there. Not only me, but my sister also – a family concern.

What an experience it was. I spent a great deal of the time biting my tongue, counting to ten and generally feeling that I was on the wrong side of the situation.

John would open the door for everyone, spend endless time searching for the right shoe, chatting and making everyone welcome.

On one occasion, at the end of my tether, and exhausted from running up and down ladders for a very rude lady, I told her that I really didn't think I could find anything that she would like.

John overheard, glared at me and took over. She eventually left satisfied and I had a long lecture on service and politeness – however rude people are. His policy was 'the ruder they are the pleasanter we are'. He reckoned they could usually be 'turned around' and he was right.

I eventually accepted this and was quite good at it. As I had very narrow feet myself I was very sympathetic to women with the same problem. In the same way, my sister always identified with wide feet and bunions! I realised years later that had I not had this experience I could never have coped with what was to come.

Chapter Two

This was now 1975. We had been in Overland Road for three years but John wanted a house in the country – preferably in the Llandeilo area. We were registered with a few estate agents who knew we wanted something quite big with some land but no one had contacted us with anything suitable.

It was during this time that a regular customer, who lived in Llandeilo came into the Mumbles shop. In conversation, we told him that we were hoping to find a large house in that area to renovate. He laughed and said, "How about the castle?"

Dynevor Castle had apparently been on the market for years.

We telephoned the agents in London instantly and arranged to meet Lord Dynevor at three o'clock the following Wednesday. We

Dynevor Castle

arrived on time but the appointment was never kept. We eventually tracked down the caretaker, showed him our appointment and he trustingly, gave us the keys.

We spent hours exploring every nook and cranny from the musty cellars to the ramparts and the lofts. What a state of excitement we were in. All John kept saying was, "Look at this, babe."

The roof was in really good repair, which was the main thing. The castle had been used latterly for concerts, and visiting artistes had used the smaller attic rooms as accommodation so even these were habitable.

One large room on the ground floor had been used as a theatre and concert hall so the ornate ceilings had been covered up to hold the lighting but underneath they were still safe and intact.

The wood, which is my joy, was wonderful everywhere and the fireplaces, door-handles, moulded ceilings, syphonic lavatories and – what impressed us as much as anything, were the brass hinges on the windows and shutters. They were six to eight inches long and as thick as my thumb. Wonderful features that are rarely seen today.

My eyes were everywhere. I reckoned I would have specially made stepladders as the ceilings were so high. One roll of wallpaper would only do two drops!

We didn't have to ask each other what we thought. We knew we wanted it. There were three cottages around the kitchen courtyard and we thought we could give free accommodation to handyman, builder or whoever else we might need.

We could borrow some money from Jo if she sold her house and moved into the flat above the Mumbles shop, which she had always wanted to do.

We found a telephone in Lord Dynevor's office and phoned Knight, Frank and Rutley, the agents.

"We'll have it," John said, but we were instantly deflated.

Having been on the market for years, it had been sold the day before privately by Lord Dynevor who had shaken hands on the deal.

We couldn't believe it – the day before! I cried with disappointment and frustration but we had to put it out of our minds.

We knew an antique dealer had bought it so at least, we thought, it would be appreciated and dealt with sympathetically. We were proved wrong.

Years later, it transpired that after various occupants nearly all the

Burry Cottage

treasures that could be removed were stripped out and sold, and latterly everything had been emulsioned – including the wonderful brass hinges.

Now, ten years later, the castle has been bought by the National Trust but too late, alas, to save the real essence of the building. They have done a lot of work to it but not with the feeling and love that we would have put into it. We could have restored it to what it used to be.

Well, from castle to cottage.

Having lived in the Mumbles house for four years, we went to look at a property in Gower. It was called 'Burry Cottage' but always known locally as 'Sydney Heath's house'.

Sydney Heath had been a well-known businessman and benefactor who had lived in Burry Cottage for many years and had created magnificent gardens – three acres of rockeries, orchard, lawns and formal gardens. It had been famous for its azaleas and rhododendrons and, although we had never seen the gardens then, they were acknowledged as probably the best in the country. Many garden parties had been held there.

We had the keys and spent time looking mainly at the house, which was very shabby but so pretty with low beams and oak floors.

Burry Cottage

There was a large stable block and a wonderful fifteenth century longhouse which had a lot of potential. John asked if I liked it and, of course, I did.

He took the keys back to the agents and I suggested he found out the exact amount of land included.

On his return he filled me in with the details, so I said, "What do you think, shall we buy it?" He gave me a sheepish look, smiled, and said, "I have."

I was amazed. We still had a lot to learn about each other. Now, I really knew he was a 'mover'. As far as he was concerned, I had said that I liked it and so did he, so let's get on with it. So we did!

This was 1976, about six years after Mr. Heath had left Gower. We bought it from his purchasers who, unfortunately, had done little or nothing in the garden, or so it would appear. Paths had disappeared, together with all the rockeries and rhododendron garden.

My mother was quite upset that we were moving so far away. She had, after my father's death in 1972, sold her house in the Uplands and moved into a lovely flat in the centre of Mumbles, so we were all quite close together. I pointed out that I would still be in the shop every day and she could come for lots of visits, which she did. All was well.

We sold our house without too much trouble and hired a van for our move. I had a Triumph Herald estate car and we did a room at a time which was quite painless.

Lil, Nellie, Pippin and Elwyn moved with us. We had somehow 'acquired' Elwyn over the last year. It had happened gradually and began with him staying the odd night. Then he had pleurisy and bronchitis very badly so we nursed him through that and he then asked if he could come with us to Gower. We questioned him about his wife but I think she'd probably put up with enough from him.

He settled in easily and had a small room of his own. He spent his evenings after a meal asleep in front of the woodstove in the kitchen. That is, until it was time to go to the pub. We had bought him an old van so he had investigated all the local hostelries; King's Head in Llangennith, Britannia in Llanmadoc, King Arthur in Reynoldston, Greyhound, Dolphin and Welcome to Town in Llanrhidian – they all knew Elwyn. His favourite was the King Arthur where he gradually spent more and more time.

We were doing our best to keep him on the straight and narrow. John had already accompanied him to court when he had quite a large bill for unpaid Income Tax. We paid this and sorted out a few other worries he had.

We paid him by the day – or rather, twice a day. This meant he had money for beer and cigarettes lunchtime and again in the evening. We didn't enjoy this but he seemed to go along with it.

We spent a year with Elwyn and Wilfred discovering the garden. It took a great deal of time and effort and every bit of our hours at home, which really were only evenings and Sundays.

Wilfred had been one of Mr. Heath's gardeners and was pleased to be back in 'his' garden. We had a great respect for him and called him 'Mr. Lucas' That was until we realised he was on Christian name terms with John. John used to say "There's something wrong here – he's Mr. Lucas and I'm John!"

Wilfred was appalled to see what had happened to the grounds in six years but worked like a Trojan and we really couldn't have managed without him.

Midge and Fountain

Eventually, we got it back, hopefully to something resembling its previous condition. I would find myself chatting away to it as I did when stripping woodwork. It demanded all our spare time. We couldn't afford to relax our labours and it began to dominate our lives.

On the main lawn was a very elegant fountain. We were devasted one morning when Wilfred told us that it had just stopped. We didn't know what to do. We knew that the garden water came from somewhere on Cefn Bryn, the hill about a mile away. In the old days there had been five water outlets in the garden; a water tap near the main lawn, two for the vegetable garden, one in the greenhouse and a little waterfall in a grotto which then formed a stream trickling into a pond. A few weeks later, we met Mr. Philpotts, a neighbour from Fairy-hill who told us that a small water spout had appeared in the middle of his parkland and he thought it could be our water pipe. We were delighted and John and Elwyn set off with spades and picks to repair it. When they eventually found the pipe about three feet below the surface, they discovered that it was asbestos and in six foot lengths. A hole had been worn in the pipe by a stone or root. As luck would have it there were some spare lengths of pipe in the longhouse so the repair was relatively easy. Because of this hole developing it had been operating on half pressure so that was probably the reason why the water could only get to the fountain. Now we had to see if it worked and we rushed back to the garden. We sat like the three monkeys and watched the fountain – our eyes glued in anticipation. We waited and waited and waited and eventually gave up – dejected. Then about three hours later a dribble appeared which, after a minute rose to about two inches. It gradually grew higher and higher. John turned the tap to its maximum and it reached fifteen feet.

This was a mistake, and the full pressure for the first time in years proved too much and must have caused another break in the pipe and we had to wait until water appeared on the surface somewhere along the run. This usually occurred at the lowest point which was somewhere on the Philpotts' land. Consequently, we became very familiar with the grounds of Fairyhill.

Over the period of about a year the pipe was to break about seven times. Some of them in hedges and most in equally inaccessible spots. It was a mammoth task. The six foot lengths were joined together with cast iron collars secured with iron bolts. We didn't have any more of these but as a long shot John visited the Water Board. He was referred to their Store which was at that time somewhere in The Strand in the centre of Swansea. An elderly storeman recognised the collar, reminisced and said he thought there were a few some-where. He eventually found them- about two dozen with the price marked two shillings and sixpence – half a crown! We bought them all – what luck!

We had, from the start, inherited Joyce from the previous owners. Joyce lived across the Green and came three mornings a week to keep us cleaned and dusted. This was a luxury, but as I was still in the Mumbles shop every day in addition to the occasional stint in the solicitors' office, it was very much appreciated.

We seemed, unintentionally, to have accumulated quite a staff around us but we all got on very well together and worked in harmony.

Midge, John and chickens

Soon after we moved in, true to form, John had been to buy some more chickens as we had left our others at Overland Road for the new owners.

There was already a chicken house up in the orchard with a proper run and high wire fence. We had twenty-four layers and later acquired guinea fowls and silkies. They had the run of the place and wandered everywhere – lawns, orchard, paddock, even down and around the house. Very tame and adventurous.

One of them absolutely refused to be locked in at night and roosted high up in a cherry tree. She reached this in various stages. First, on to a low wall, to a flower pot then a fluttery leap to the lowest branch. She would make her way high up into the tree and on a windy night really had to hang on. She was quite a character and would come into the kitchen through the cat flap. We felt she deserved an identity so John christened her 'Martha Gatwick'. We considered her more of a pet.

We were quite self-sufficient once we organised ourselves. There was a large greenhouse where we had replaced thirty-five panes of glass. We grew tomatoes and cucumbers of course, and also planted a vine. We had aubergines, peppers and chillies as well as experimental things like vegetable spaghetti and physalis. I started off all seedlings ready for planting out.

There was a netted fruit garden where we had planted all the berries: blackcurrants, redcurrants, strawberries, raspberries, gooseberries and also a fig tree that was just beginning to produce a reasonable amount when we left.

In the vegetable plot we grew potatoes, runner beans, broad beans, carrots, cauliflowers, cabbage, peas, mange-tout, sprouts, parsnips and broccoli. This patch of garden was so big that our next door neighbour came in to plough it for us. I had also taken great pains with an asparagus bed which was also coming good when we left.

Between the fruit, vegetables, eggs, lambs and chickens, there wasn't much we had to buy. I had also taught myself to spin and once I had perfected the technique of spinning wool, I moved on to doghair. This was wonderful when spun into yarn and I made myself the most amazing coat. Everyone loved it and customers in the shop wanted one. I couldn't possibly spin and knit this yarn, it would take too long but it did get me started on knitting mohair coats for the shop which were very successful and almost our best sellers. I must have sold dozens over the years.

We were going through a terrible episode with our domestic pets. Nellie, one of the cats was run over outside the house one evening.

Vegetable garden and orchard with chickens

Reclaimed rockery

Lillian had picked up poison and died and now poor old Pippin had reached the age of fourteen and was slowing down. He was also deaf and half blind. Life was becoming hard work and after a great deal of heart searching, we arranged for his final departure and asked the vet to come to the house. I was devastated to lose him. He had seen me through a lot of ups and downs and had been a great friend. We buried him at the top of the garden next to Lil, Nellie and two black cats we had inherited from the previous owners. They all had headstones and it was beginning to resemble Boot Hill.

A few months later we acquired a wonderful collie puppy called 'Caleb' We had him for three years when he suddenly disappeared. We came home one day and he had gone. We searched and advertised and cried. We never saw him again but never got over the pain of wondering what could have happened. It was an agonising time which we still find difficult to talk about.

I loved Burry Cottage and was happy there. It had a wonderful 'feel' and its large, low-ceilinged rooms were both spacious and cosy. We put in three woodburning stoves so the house smelled wonderful inside and out. The only fault was that although we had all the lovely gardens, they were at the back of the house where we couldn't see them. All we had in the front was the road. A house in the middle of its own grounds would be ideal – a house like Fairyhill!

Fairyhill was only a quarter of a mile from Burry Cottage and we knew the grounds well because, as I have said, the pipe supplying our garden water came from Cefn Bryn passing through Fairyhill.

We had met the couple who owned it, and indeed had been invited to their Ruby Wedding party. They had bought it thirty-five years previously when it had already begun its slow decline and by this time they were living in about two of the rooms, all the others being firmly shuttered.

Their electricity was produced by a generator run on diesel. Indeed, on one occasion, when all of Gower was snowed in, we carried diesel and candles down to them. They were huddled in their sitting room with a bucket catching the rain water. Their water supply also came from Cefn Bryn with the reservoir very close to ours.

The night of the party must have been one of the few times that the two main gates were opened. They were always firmly closed and bolted making it impossible to see into the house and grounds.

On this occasion, all the rooms were open and we were able to look around. The Philpotts said that we were welcome to explore but only to put the lights on as we needed them as the generator couldn't cope with many.

It was an enjoyable evening and we met some very old local people with interesting tales to tell.

In the large drawing room the carpet had been removed for dancing but people sat around the walls in straight backed chairs, the men with starched collars. One old chap even had a butterfly collar. Everything was in half light and the atmosphere damp and musty. A three piece 'band' stood in the corner of the room and John was convinced he could see cobwebs on the violin!

A buffet had been laid out in the billiard room which was lit with candles. There were no other lights. The floor was very uneven with a lot of holes and quite rotten. The walls appeared to be wood-panelled although it was really too dark to tell. I could just about see

Longhouse form south side

Longhouse from garden side

John at the end of the room, smiling to himself. He thought that the faded and worn velvet curtains were pale pink with a grey stripe. The grey turned out to be a thick layer of dust on the folds. He wandered away muttering something about 'Great Expectations'.

The only rooms furnished were the sitting room and the bedroom where they slept. Various pieces of antique furniture were standing about in the halls and corridors. I remember a bearskin rug in the front hall which people must have been tripping over for years as half its teeth had been knocked out!

On opening the door to the very largest bedroom we were amazed to find it elegantly furnished with a huge four poster bed whose canopy stretched right up to the extremely high ceiling. It was such a surprise having passed through bare floored corridors and so many empty, echoing rooms. We thought the bed must be worth a fortune, but why not sell it and do some repairs?

It was a few years later that we learned that Fairyhill was on the market but at a ridiculously high price. In the owners' eyes it was still the grand house of fifty years ago and nothing would convince them otherwise. We were forced to put it out of our minds.

We had been in Burry Cottage for about six years and John decided he wanted a change. He was now fifty-five and had been in the shop for forty-two years. His brother, who was ten years younger and had a lot less 'service' than John was also there but they had never really seen eye to eye. John worked more by flair and instinct whereas his brother was meticulously into bookwork and stock control. It should have made an ideal team but somehow it didn't work.

John decided to buy out his brother and we had already found an alternative shop premises in the new Quadrant Shopping Centre which was far more central than the Kingsway.

As it happened, his brother retaliated with an alternative offer – him buying out John. It really didn't matter to John – he just wanted to do his own thing.

We had it in our minds to buy a bigger boat and sail the world. This would mean selling Burry Cottage and buying a small property as a base. We weren't totally committed to this idea but it was a possibility. John had another notion of buying a pub but on this score my foot came very firmly down. No way did I want to be tied every afternoon and evening.

We were in a state of indecision. Twice we heard that people had bought Fairyhill. For a year we all but forgot it and delved into various other schemes. John's enthusiasm desperately needed channelling.

We thought we might turn our large stable block into a cottage for self catering. We had already done this to our longhouse and that was very successful. We even thought of bed and breakfast in Burry Cottage. Everything we pursued came to nothing.

At this time Fairyhill had, so we thought, been sold and in fact a large auction of its contents were to be held in a marquee in the grounds. This took place the week after John had finished in the shop, October 1982, and we walked down to the sale. It was a depressing day with drizzle and low cloud which did nothing to enhance the desperate appearance of Fairyhill. The house was so dark with its shutters closed that hardly anything could be seen.

Half of Gower were there. It was a good social event but we didn't buy anything. Most things were sold although they couldn't have been in a very good condition. The four poster bed fetched nine thousand pounds and someone even bought the toothless bearskin rug!

Our days became more leisurely and we promised ourselves that we would walk and explore every part of Gower.

It was on returning from one of these walks, coming through Fairyhill lane, that we saw two people in the grounds. "Who's that?" says John. "Damned cheek, being in there."

We had always considered the grounds as ours. I said that perhaps they were looking with a view to buying as I had very recently seen another sale advertisement in the local paper.

We both fell very quiet and I knew what he was thinking. Neither of us spoke but continued our way home.

I knew what he was going to do and sure enough, I was right. Straight on the telephone to discover the asking price. It had dropped dramatically. Apparently, heaps of people wanted it but couldn't get a loan or mortgage because of the terrible state of repair

I don't think we even discussed it. I just know when something is right. We went straight to the Philpotts' solicitors (would you believe?)

as our solicitor was away and we not only signed the contract but also exchanged, and Fairyhill was ours! On his return, our solicitor was cross and told me I should know better – I'd worked for him long enough. No searches – no surveys!

Well, we knew everything was wrong with it, so what was the point. That's why no one else had bought it – too frightened!

This was the end of January 1983 and completion would be on 1st May.

The excitement was intense. But what had we done? We now had two houses. Things would work out, we knew. Hadn't Fairyhill waited for us? A whole year. Although we had tried to put it out of our minds, nothing else we planned had worked out – fate indeed.

Fairyhill had already taken on a personality to me. As I had talked encouragingly to the garden at Burry Cottage, so I talked to Fairyhill. Hadn't it rejected all other would-be purchasers and hung on for us? Brave Fairyhill, just wait and see what we will do for you in return. Brace yourself for the onslaught – new roofs and floors. Everything will be uncovered, inspected and lovingly repaired. I'm sure your wood is beautiful but what little paint there is needs burning off, cleaning and feeding. You will soon be alive and proud again.

This all sounds very melodramatic but it's how I felt. Our dream was to bring back the glorious days when it was splendid, with stables, walled gardens, parks, lake and trout stream. Could we do it? Yes!

Chapter Three

It was a long wait from January to May 1983 but we had a house to sell and another to investigate. During this long wait I set out to delve into the past and explore the last two hundred and sixty years. It appears that as far back as 1705 the estate was owned by a John Lucas (no relation to Wilfred) who lived in Stouthall, about two miles away. It was probably called Ferney Cross Hill at that time and gradually changed over the years.

John Lucas apparently bequeathed Ferney Hill estate to his younger son, Richard and a house was built on it for him in 1720 and called 'Peartree'.

After Richard's death his son John, who was the Vicar of Usk came to live there with his wife. This would have been 1765 and they were there for nineteen years before moving to Cheriton, about four miles away in the north of Gower. His sister lived there and was also married to a vicar.

This was now 1784 and yet another John Lucas, a younger son of the Stouthall branch of the family moved in with his wife. They only stayed for three years as his father died, so he returned to inherit the main family home at Stouthall. This was the go-ahead Lucas who liked change – he dropped the name 'Peartree' so it became just Fairyhill. He also totally renovated Stouthall, enlarging and improving it to a very elegant mansion, much larger and grander than Fairyhill.

Between this time and 1814 the house was let on two separate occasions to London businessmen. It would be interesting to know the rent charged.

I was enjoying this research. It was all adding an identity to Fairyhill. Visualising the different people there all those years ago. Incredible that the original design of the house had hardly been changed.

Diana, Baroness Barham was the next person to lease from the Lucas family. She was a very religious lady and was led to Gower by God to save the heathens. In nine years she had built and started up

*Portrait of John Lucas, painted 1788, kindly given to me
by Mr. Robert Lucas of Reyndoldston*

six chapels and numerous schools. The chapels were Bethesda in Burry Green, Trinity in Cheriton, Bethel in Penclawdd, Emmanuel in Pitton Green then further to Ilston and as far away as Paraclete in Newton.

She was well-respected and entered into the community doing a great deal of good works.

Stories of her stay in Gower are related in a lot of books and she made quite an impact. She had apparently been carried to and from Bethesda Chapel in Burry Green by sedan chair!

She died at Fairyhill in 1823 and her body was taken all the way back to Kent, the hearse being drawn by six black, plumed horses. It must have taken weeks.

Now, the last Lucas to reside at the house took occupation. Henry was very flamboyant and a great gambler. He owned a string of race-horses which were exercised on Cefn Bryn daily. I suppose these would have been housed in the home farm across the road from the main house as the stable would have held the coach horses,

He was an extravagant man and was soon overtaken by debt. Fairyhill, together with his estate in Cheriton had to be sold and he moved to Swansea. He had been at Fairyhill for only five years. This was now 1828.

It remained empty for four years until the Reverend Samuel Phillips, who was Curate of Llanmadoc, Llangennith and Llandewi bought it. He had been in love with Lady Barham's daughter whom he had met when she lived at Fairyhill. She really loved the place. She always called it 'Fairyland' and was sad to leave it when her mother died.

They married in 1834 so she was pleased to be back. They were there twenty years and, in fact, they both died the same year- 1855 – absolutely broke. There was an auction to raise money. Apparently, the servants hadn't been paid for ten years! This was the second occupant to have money problems.

Once again, the house lay empty for three years before the Benson family took ownership. Firstly, Starling Benson, one time Mayor of Swansea and a great philanthropist.

He died a bachelor and in 1879 it passed to his brother, General Henry Roxby Benson and his family.

General Benson was the brother-in-law of Matthew Arnold, the poet who visited Fairyhill with his family in this same year. We often were to wonder which room he slept in.

Portrait of Anne of Cheriton painted about 1770

Bensons at Fairyhill 1880's

It seems to be the daughter of General Benson who made a big impression on the area. Buying books for the Sunday school, running fetes, providing 'sumptuous' teas, supplying flowers and labour to decorate Reynoldston church, funding outings, supplying coal to the needy and teaching at Sunday school.

We know that up until this time there would have been about twenty-three servants employed at Fairyhill. Probably half of them at least were garden and farm workers.

We could imagine the outside workers gathering in the Bothey House. The huge bell that hung on the pine end of the kitchen wing rang at eight o'clock in the morning, midday and four o'clock to signify meal times. The Bothey house, which is still in the courtyard has a fireplace downstairs so it would have been warm at all times, There was an outside lavatory by the Coach House solely for the workers. Probably a great luxury for them in those days, provided by a thoughtful employer.

One of the Benson sisters, Margaret, was the last to leave Fairyhill in 1921. An elderly local resident told us that he can remember when he was a little boy seeing her carriage driving through the lanes.

A carriageway used to run parallel with the road at Fairyhill. It ran from the Coach House, around the front of the house, down through

Bensons at Fairyhill 1880's

Drawing room at Fairyhill 1880's

the woods, and came out through gates on the cross roads. The gateway can still be seen today but has been walled up for years.

The new owner, Percy Rowlands, continued the Benson tradition and in the first year of his occupation held a fête in the grounds to raise money for a new village hall in Reynoldston. It was very popular, with dancing on the lawn. What a lovely idea. Perhaps we could do it. In those days there were no parking problems and not so much rain.

He stayed for only eight years before he too ran into money problems and had to sell up. Was there a curse on Fairyhill? He was the third to go through and, we hoped, the last!

This brings us to 1929 and Tom Harris, a Swansea solicitor. He stayed for about eighteen years and was the last to enjoy the lifestyle of a country gentleman. For Fairyhill it was now all downhill.

The people that we bought from had lived there for thirty-five years and let it deteriorate. Both house and grounds were almost beyond any human help.

My mother, who loved Burry Cottage and delighted in its comfort on her many visits, was distraught when I told her we had bought Fairyhill. She couldn't believe that we wanted to take on such a task, forfeiting the luxury we had for a ruin. "Why not buy Oystermouth Castle?" she asked caustically, "That only needs a new roof".

It caused a rift between us and I didn't see her for many months. She was upset enough to move in with my sister for a couple of weeks when poor Jo had to deal with her anger!

I didn't know how to cope with this. She hadn't even been inside Fairyhill but knew of it. We had walked past on many occasions. Not that anything could be seen from the road. The gates were very high and hedgerows so overgrown – it was quite impenetrable. Some inquisitive people, thinking the place to be abandoned, would climb in and try to peer through the shuttered windows. Rumour has it that some had been threatened with a shotgun but I can't honestly vouch for the truth of that!

Burry Cottage was put on the market. There was an initial rush of interest which soon lapsed. We had far too much on our minds to worry about it. We had to get on!

Quickly! – open every door and shutter. Let the air and the sunshine in. Let's get rid of the mustiness and damp smell. We hadn't seen it in daylight and it was even more horrifying.

So what to do about builders? We didn't want a firm of contractors. This was our project and we wanted to go slowly and enjoy it. A step at a time, feeling our way. If we sold Burry Cottage we could camp somewhere. There was no rush, we were just going to live in it.

Elwyn had left us about a year previously. He had been persuaded to do some work for a man in Reynoldston who, of course, had paid him. This meant that he was soon on whisky in addition to beer and didn't want the restriction of us nagging him. He left to live in a caravan in the car park of the King Arthur and this was to be his downfall. Nothing we could say would stop him. No one now to clothe him and see that he ate three meals a day. He only lasted a few years and was to die more or less alone. I suppose it was bound to happen sooner or later. Now that we had Fairyhill we were so wishing he was still with us. He would have enjoyed it.

Fairyhill 1880's

We heard about Frank from friends of ours who own an hotel in Swansea – Pam and Ron Rumble. He had done some good work for them and they were pleased.

Frank came to see us. A quiet, Welsh-speaking man of middle years who talked very quickly with a cigarette permanently stuck to his lip and, quite honestly, neither of us could catch much of what he said.

He seemed totally undaunted by the state of the place or the size. Most people had told us to knock it down and we were delighted by Frank's optimism. Not for him the demolition of the old outbuildings which were already roofless and, very nearly, wall-less!

"We'll fix that." – Music to my ears.

The billiard room, which had been added to the house a little later was very bad and some friends had almost panicked us into believing it would have to come down. Frank said quietly, "Soon put that right – nothing to worry about."

I remember we called in Rentokil for a survey. I particularly told the surveyor not to go to the billiard room. We knew that was bad and we intended totally gutting it and replacing floors and maybe windows. This would enable us to completely overhaul the cellar which was directly underneath.

I left him to it at half past nine in the morning and ran into him about lunchtime. I asked him how he was getting on. He had ignored my instructions and said, "I've just finished the billiard room and that alone will cost you five thousand pounds for treatment!"

Now that Frank had been found we had to wait a few weeks before he could start.

John had already begun outside. We had to hack through undergrowth and remove fallen trees just to delineate the paths. Originally, there had been a walk the whole length of the trout stream. Now we could hardly make out the water.

This stream was the Burry Pill that came underground from Brecon and rose at Llandewi. It made its way down to Cheriton passing through Fairyhill. At one time this tiny length of river ran no less than seven water mills.

There was no electricity at Fairyhill and we had investigated the possibility of a water wheel. The force of water coming over the weir was quite strong enough to drive one. We didn't pursue the idea very far as apparently, we would have to pay for the use of the water as it passed by the wheel. It appears there is no easy way of doing anything.

South outlook when we bought

39

Looking down same view from house

Looking out from the front of the house which, incidentally, faces south like any self-respecting mansion, the 'lawn' was narrow and led down to a ha-ha across the parkland. It was flanked by thick under-growth and overgrown rhododendrons.

I must say now, that although I have the vision to see houses completed, John is the one who can organise the grounds and he could see straight away what was needed.

My friend Joyce, had come down from London for a holiday – some hope. She was soon roped in. We cut back the rhodos on the left of the lawn. These had encroached at least fifteen yards and also grown high up and across the east wing of the house, totally covering the windows of the ground and first floors. Inside too, where the windows were broken.

While Joyce and I were still clearing the rhododendrons, John was on the right hand side of the lawn pulling out dead trees, bushes and brambles. These were hauled out by the winch on our trusty Land Rover and very gradually we uncovered the trees that now make the feature of the whole outlook, including a magnificent copper beech which seems to frame the house as seen from the park. We unearthed slowly the path leading down to the park and later made a bridge

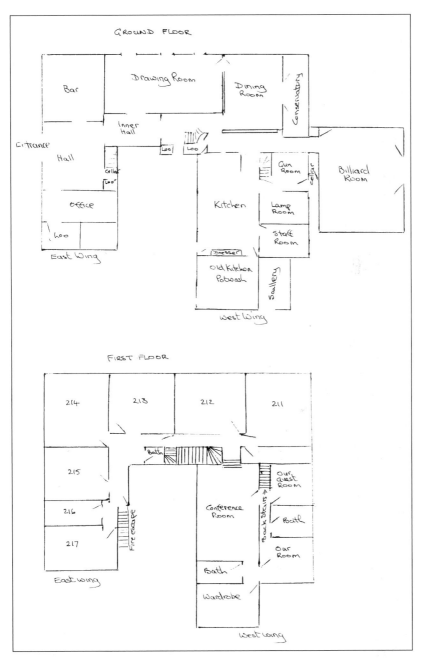

Plan of house lay-out

41

across the ha-ha. What excitement when we revealed a sweet chest-nut tree with its wonderful rutted bark!

Everything was discovery. Rather like Burry Cottage – only more.

We seemed to have bonfires for ever and need I say it? The weather was the hottest for years. Temperatures in the eighties and we had been stoking. We had bonfire burn, not sunburn!

John, Joyce and I would crawl back to Burry Cottage for a bath, a meal and a nice bottle of wine and look forward to the next day. Now that the undergrowth had been cleared in that part, from the house we could look down to the park through the newly exposed trees. The lawn had quadrupled in size. The shutters and windows were open and we could almost feel Fairyhill taking its first deep breath in years.

The shape of the house was like the letter 'E' without the middle bit. The main front part consisted of a hall, library, drawing room with adjoining door to dining room, conservatory and billiard room. Above, were four bedrooms on the first floor and four bedrooms in the attic. The attic was frighteningly bad and had been occupied by birds and bats for years. Some of the servants probably lived up there as it was such a climb up narrow winding stairs.

The east wing consisted of the hall downstairs, breakfast room and sewing room. Above was a long passageway with four rooms leading off.

The west wing was totally derelict apart from the kitchen and house-keeper's pantry on the ground floor. These led off a long pass-ageway at the end of which was the original old kitchen with earth floor, open to the roof, and lean-to scullery.

Leading off to the left of this passageway – passing the row of brass bells which were, at one time, connected to all rooms – were, or what used to be the lamp room, gun room, storeroom and dairy. The lamp and gun rooms were buried under rubble that had been the up-stairs of this wing.

To investigate above the kitchen, we had to secure parts of the floor to enable us to walk safely. Then we could see that there was a passageway directly above the downstairs passageway with four small servants' rooms leading off to the right.

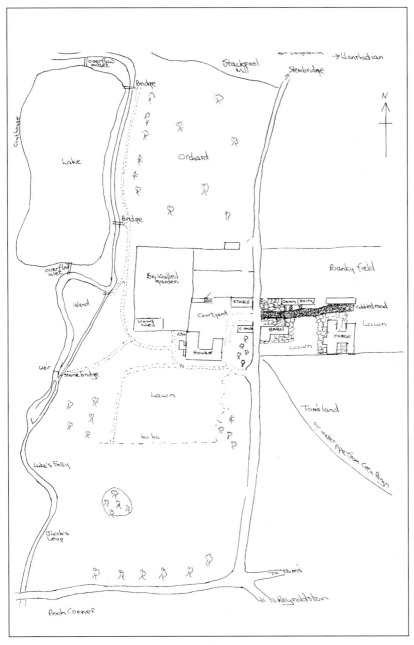

Plan of Grounds

Through a door on the left were four more small rooms. A back stairs, which was now non-existent had led down to the kitchen.

There were three high-walled gardens, the largest of which had been for vegetables. It had been laid out with proper paths and we could see what remained of the box hedges that lined them.

One of the smaller gardens had a nectarine house which, alas, would have bankrupted us to repair. The peach and nectarine still survived but unfortunately, were cut through by someone who dismantled the frame for us. This was very sad as it must have really struggled to survive for so many years.

Through this walled garden, heading North, we came to the remains of many greenhouses. These must have been heated because in the middle was a boiler house, fallen in, of course. We wondered how long since they were in use. Someone told us that the Philpotts', who had a flower shop, had used them, but I don't know for certain. It doesn't take very long for a garden and glasshouses to become overgrown and past the point of repair.

The orchard was beyond the greenhouses but most of the trees were dead and on the ground. We had so much wood for our stoves. Some cooking apples survived and various eaters but the fruit was all badly marked and the trees needed a lot of attention. I was delighted to find a very small russet tree – my favourite apple!

Past the orchard and across the stream was mostly water meadow and very difficult to explore – impossible in wet weather.

It was all very daunting and I left John to it. I knew my place – in the home!

We had bought Fairyhill purely for the challenge of rescuing it and keeping ourselves occupied. There was to be no rush and no pressure. After all, John had retired, hadn't he?

We thought we would start at one end – the conservatory. We could put a woodstove there, keep warm and work our way along from that end. We would probably only do the downstairs and first floor and leave the attics and the upstairs of the derelict west wing till a later date. Everything was very leisurely and we were having a ball.

Chapter Four

It was sometime about now that I was hearing the odd remark from John about making Fairyhill into an hotel. I was not amused. He said we were spending too much money. I suggested doing bed and breakfast, sharing Fairyhill with a few privileged visitors from Easter through the summer. I thought that would be very satisfactory without too much stress. It would be an ideal life – the whole summer going flat out in a business we could both enjoy and we would have the winter to recover, have a holiday and prepare for the next season.

I know John when he gets the bit between his teeth – he's swept along with his own enthusiasm and can see all the good things that can happen. We usually see eye to eye with each other's ideas and rarely argue about important issues. As John sees the advantages in any project so the disadvantages leap out at me. I tend to look for the snags in any situation and visualise what could go wrong. In that way I feel I can anticipate any mistakes. I worry and delve into any prospective venture until I'm sure of what is ahead. Now, in the situation that was manifesting itself into an all-consuming passion with John, snags were leaping at me from all directions. I could see the long hours and the endless late nights. The tiredness making us irritable and quarrelsome. A divorce possibly?

All my arguments were dismissed with ease – this from a man who was a rotten sleeper and who had to be in bed straight after 'News at Ten'!

We went to dinner with our hotelier friends, Ron and Pam, who ran a very successful business, Windsor Lodge Hotel. This did more to fire John and a general feeling of enthusiasm dominated the evening. Ron's encouragement to go ahead completely swamped my arguments. I was attacked from both sides and told that my whole attitude was 'blinkered' and that I should investigate all options. I was lost!

John was now 'full pelt'. He first of all approached the Tourist Board

Wet walls to Billiard Room

"After"

to see what was available in the way of a Grant. We were soon given the cold shoulder there and told we couldn't have anything as we had already made a start by replacing guttering.

Looking back on this years later, it always seemed an irony as the Welsh Tourist Board held us up as an example and brought many official visitors to show them what could be done.

I really didn't mind that we failed to have a Grant as now we weren't restricted or told what we could or couldn't do. I had a very clear idea of what we wanted and didn't fancy all the form filling and permissions.

Very soon we had a visit from an architect, another friend of Ron's. If this was going to proceed we had to have bathrooms to every bedroom and plans had to be submitted for planning permission.

A Planning Officer arrived and then one morning when we were driving into Fairyhill I saw stuck to the gate – horror of horrors – a Notice informing all and sundry that Fairyhill was to be an hotel. I was not ready for this and very upset. I felt that everything had been taken out of my hands and somehow gone out of control.

Worse was to come. On returning to Burry Cottage that evening, a reporter telephoned from the 'Evening Post' for a full story. Exactly what were we planning, and did the area need this? More to the point, did I need this?

John talked to him while I was shouting down the stairs about suing if he wrote anything.

Poor John, I know he would have enjoyed expanding on his plans but I wasn't ready to share this thing with the world. I had to get used to the idea.

I felt quite drained emotionally and couldn't face Fairyhill for a few days. I relaxed in the tranquillity of Burry Cottage and tanned my body in the sun!

Frank had now got started. He had arrived with Martin and the two of them got stuck in straight away. Martin was in his twenties and years younger than Frank but also extremely quiet. Nevertheless, I was very impressed as he seemed to understand everything Frank said. He was to be the interpreter!

Conservatory before we started

It seemed a lot of work for two of them and they said they would need a labourer. This turned out to be Roddy who was super – and actually spoke. John had had it in the back of his mind that he would be able to do the labouring, but later on when he saw Roddy running up planks with a barrow load of cement he was relieved he hadn't suggested it.

The first job to be done was to stop the water coming in so we had started on the guttering. Most of this was non-existent so it was a vast job. We went to a builders' merchants with Frank's order for gutters and downpipes and were asked if we were building a housing estate. The questioner was serious!

The house inside was so wet everywhere that it was going to take months to dry out. Luckily, the summer of 1983 was hot so we were able to keep everything open.

The shutters that were on all windows, except the attic, had been closed permanently so there had been no sunshine in the rooms at all. Everything smelt musty and looked damp. What little wallpaper there was had mostly peeled off. All, that is, except in the billiard room. We thought, in the half light that this was wood-panelled but it was very thick paper painted to look like wood. I think it must have been stuck on with glue and it was too thick to soak off. I managed to remove about three feet at a time. It took many days.

Once the paper was removed, a concealed door was revealed – a secret passage leading to treasure, obviously! No such luck – just an alcove where the billiard cues had been kept, Before resealing it we left a 'time capsule'. General information of who we were and what we were doing, together with some newspapers, coins and various bits and pieces that amused us.

My mother was back on the scene again after ignoring me for months and was helping with the removal of wallpaper and other selective jobs. John and I had been decorating the sitting room in her flat. John emulsioning the ceiling and me wallpapering. She seemed to have accepted the fact that we had bought Fairyhill but still thought it a mistake.

The park beyond the front lawn, leading down to the river was becoming very overgrown and needed grazing. We asked Colin Davies, a neighbouring farmer if he would like to put some horses in and he was delighted. Two mares arrived and seemed to settle quite soon. They must have been there about a month when one morning John came up to Burry Cottage specially to tell me that the grey had foaled. I dropped everything and back we went. What a dear little thing, only hours old and wobbling. I immediately christened it Pixie as it was born in Fairyhill but then we noticed this was a mistake and changed the name to Hobgoblin – Hobby for short. I felt great possessiveness towards him although I knew he was nothing to do with me. We chatted every day and it was lovely to look down from the house, across the ha-ha and watch the mares and foal wandering about.

A few weeks later we attended our local Pony Show in Llangennith, where John was President that year, and we were chatting to Colin Davies. I told him about Hobby and how super he was. He knew about him and told us that, in fact, he had been in to catch him and his mum and taken them away. Oh, what a shock. I felt really cheated!

John in conservatory ready for action

After renovation

Having got the roof and gutters sorted out, we made a start on rebuilding the conservatory. This was rotten and had to be taken down. It had, at some time been heated by water coming from a boiler directly below in the cellar and had gigantic pipes around the walls.

We wanted to rebuild it in exactly the same way. An enormous amount of wood arrived, enough to rebuild the conservatory and repair the glass rooflight of the billiard room. New panels had to be made. This proved to be quite a big job and it was at this early stage that I learnt to glaze. Martin showed me and off I went. My fingers became marked with tiny cuts which soon filled with putty.

I managed to bed the glass onto the putty well enough but it took me longer to master the nailing and sealing in of the glass. Doing the basic job was alright but putting just the right thickness so that the putty didn't show through to the inside took me a while. Practice makes perfect and having started on the conservatory and then completing the rest of the sixty-six windows in the house, I reckon I had mastered it!

Hugh, our next door neighbour at Stackpole Mill had asked if we needed any help and started off by rebuilding a stone pillar for another new gate into the park. He is quite clever and seems able to turn his hand to anything. His little boy, Andrew, appears to accompany him at all times. Hugh is an engineer who prefers leading a full but stress-free life in the country to working in industry.

He approached John to ask if he could possibly work full-time at Fairyhill with Frank, Martin and Roddy. He would be wonderful to have around and it would mean having someone on the spot for any jobs we might need. Could we afford him? Sell Burry Cottage first, then we'll think again.

I suppose the bats had been in residence for so long that they thought they had the run of the place. One lived under the stairs between the dining room and the kitchen. Doubtless there were more there but only one at a time appeared. I named it 'Emily' and I called to her "Coming through Em" as I shot past in the half light with my head down. We soon got used to her.

Celyn as a puppy

As I said, there was no electricity at Fairyhill. We struggled with the generator but it couldn't cope with Martin's drill, cement mixer and the kettle. Once it got dark, we had to go home.

We were still living at Burry Cottage with Winni and went back there every evening tired and generally filthy. The following morning we were up early and back down to meet the men at eight o'clock. We were to continue living in Burry Cottage for another year.

Six months after starting work on Fairyhill, Guinevere, a friend of ours who lives in London but has a holiday home in Llangennith, called on us carrying a little furry bundle under her coat. She had found the stray puppy in Penrice on her way to Oxwich. She told us it had shown up in her headlights and on investigating found it cold and shaking curled around some pony droppings for warmth!

She knew we had lost Caleb the year before and this was very like him – a cross collie bitch.

It's never the right time to have a puppy but this really threw me. Of course, I adored her on sight but puppies take a lot of training early on and there was nothing for it but to take a week off and stay at home.

She was the sweetest thing and I called her 'Celyn'. I had never heard of anyone called this. It means 'holly' in Welsh and I liked the sound of it. Many people have since copied it.

She was unbelievably clever, as are most collies, and was trained in no time. John took her on to Burry Green where she, of course, started to chase the sheep. This is what he wanted and he struck her quite hard with a stick. He hated doing this but it's the only way to teach dogs not to chase and she never forgot her lesson.

She was carried to Fairyhill everyday stuffed down my thermal zipper jacket and amused herself with everyone, picking up tools and brushes and generally driving us crazy! I had to keep up the training and took her out for "Wee-wee please, Celyn" every hour. This was

Celyn helping to strip a shutter. Still growing into her ears!

53

very time consuming but she soon learnt and knew which door to go to. Everyone loved her and still does.

My godson, Luke, came to stay with us at this time. He was Joyce's son and she wanted him to have some country air, a change from London. Although he was fourteen it was the first time he had stayed away from home on his own and Joyce was afraid he would be homesick. She thought he might only manage a couple of days and I promised to put him on the train if I thought he was unhappy.

He was a quiet, sensitive boy but very easy to get along with. He brought his dog, Jake with him and fortunately Jake and Celyn became good friends.

Luke had a wonderful time and really blossomed. He worked with the builders, barrowing rubble, driving the tractor and generally labouring.

He took some time off and he and Andrew made a raft out of oil drums and wood. It took them all day and we all went down beyond the park, over the water meadow to the deepest part of the river where it was launched with great ceremony. Luke and Andrew both lowered themselves on to it from a tree and it slowly but surely sank! This part of the stream we called 'Luke's Folly'.

Further up the river where Jake the dog had fallen in and failed to scrabble up the steep sides of the bank we called 'Jacob's Leap'. I had to wade in and lift him out. It's easy to see how places get their names.

Luke had been with us for about six weeks when his mother came down from London to see what he'd been up to. She was missing him and wanted him back. By this time he had changed from a lanky, pale boy into a sun-tanned youth with muscles! It was a lovely summer.

One afternoon when John was out by the front gate clearing the driveway, a German family stopped to ask where they could find accommodation. It was a bank holiday and everywhere was full and they were desperate.

John found me and said, "We'll have a practice run and do the bed and breakfast at home". My mind went instantly to the state of the house and the bedrooms and I said, "O.K. but I need two hours". What a scamper. Up to Burry Cottage to sort out the beds and generally tidy up!

There were five of them – two double bedrooms and a single. What a hoot! Next morning I cooked the breakfast and John served them. They thought it was wonderful – and so did we!

We were having a struggle to get the electricity. The nearest sub-station was about a quarter of a mile away at 'Pooh Corner'. This was what we called the Water Board's Treatment Works near the south boundary of our grounds. An unfair name but, it amused us.

The surveyors eventually arrived, measured and worked out how many poles were required and where they would be sited. I couldn't believe it when they said they would bring the poles straight up the middle of the park!

John pointed out that it would ruin the view and that electricity poles were not things of beauty, but as far as they were concerned, that was the shortest route. For this, they wanted five thousand pounds, which was a lot of money in 1983.

Eventually, we persuaded them to take a longer route starting with two poles further down towards the river and then we would hire a machine and dig a trench alongside the path in the woods right up to the conservatory and into the cellar. It was a lot more expensive but we couldn't have tolerated the alternative. People are too quick to take the easy option.

Having finished the conservatory, we used it as a room where I could work on my wood. The windows, John would remove, at first with Martin's help but he was soon able to cope on his own. Then I would remove the glass panes carefully. Some of them were very thin and warped but I tried to save them all. Of course, I did break some which had to be replaced with new glass. I used my small gas blow lamp to burn off what little paint there was then scrubbed the wood with a solution of water and caustic soda. Having washed this off thoroughly with lots of cold water, I left it for a few days to dry.

The hardest part then was the sanding down of the wood. This

Midge "stripping" dining room doors

After completion

took the longest time of all but I kept telling myself it would all be worth the effort. To finish it, I used a wood dye and two coats of sealer, sanded again between each coat. The outside would then have two coats of white paint and it would be ready for glazing. There were windows in various stages of treatment all around the house. A lot of the hardwood sills had to be renewed and I painted all the frames before John replaced the sashes.

In addition to this almost full time work at Fairyhill, we also had to keep the gardens at Burry Cottage under control. Wilfred was there but it needed us for the constant weeding and general tender loving care. If we wanted to sell, it had to be maintained. We couldn't spoil all the hard work it had taken to reclaim it from the wilderness we had inherited.

As the weather got colder, we lit the woodstove in the conservatory. This was one we had put in the greenhouse in Burry Cottage. It was a huge pot bellied stove which burnt absolutely anything and it kept us warm all through the winter. We called it 'Puff'.

All the visitors sat in the conservatory. There was nowhere else safe. Floors were up, walls were down and stairs were out.

Things were coming along slowly. We had another joiner by the name of Mark and we all worked well together. They seemed to accept me as 'one of the boys'. We would discuss the plan of campaign and analyse every new job before it was started. They were very good and patient with me if I had a sudden change of idea. They tackled jobs they had never come across before and consequently, I'm sure, learnt a great deal.

They had by this time, completed the conservatory, dining room and drawing room and were in the front hall area. To the left of this hall was the library. I had wanted the door moved. We blocked up the original one in the inner hall and built a new one leading in from the main hall, near the front door. We made this new door with a bevelled glass top to match the front door so now we had a little more light in the hall. The old library was to be the bar. I designed the actual bar and Martin did a brilliant job building it out of old doors, shutters and spindles. For the counter he used Douglas fir which I sanded within an inch of its life and gave about ten coats of varnish.

Underneath the bar was a cellar which would be perfect for the beer. It was a huge cellar and we also put a sauna down there.

Leading from the hall to the inner hall was a very narrow doorway and I wanted this widened and left as an open arch, matching some arched alcoves further down the hallway.

This area now looked terrible and no one could use the front door. The whole floor of the bar and hallway was non existent. It proved to be rotten and had to be replaced so we were balancing on planks.

While doing this, Martin discovered a wonderful wooden beam which was used as a lintel below the floor of the doorway we were widening. We replaced this with a bigger steel lintel and after a lot of hard work we were to use this lovely old beam above the woodstove in the hall.

Bar "before"

Bar made from doors and shutters

The telephone was connected but we needed a few more additional ones. Until the engineers came to do this, the solitary telephone was in the inner hall on the window sill. This meant we couldn't hear it ringing if we were at the other end of the house. The only one with good enough ears was Celyn, so when we saw her get up and run, someone always ran after her to answer it. She thought it a great game.

When we had our extra points installed, the phone would ring in three different places and we would all be running in different directions. It was hilarious – us running and Celyn barking. She does it to this day!

The next part the builders went to was the worst – above the kitchen. It had been blocked off from the main house as it had fallen in and was so dangerous. It had to be totally gutted. What had been a passageway and four bedrooms we thought could be a huge bedroom and bathroom for us. This would also have two guest bedrooms for friends, with separate bathrooms in place of the original four small rooms the other side of the passageway.

The back stairs had long since fallen in and we had to move across by walking on planks. Martin had to make new stairs. The bottom three steps were usable and stayed in place but the whole flight took a lot of building and fitting as the walls were so uneven.

In one of the old rooms buried under the rubble was a wonderful old bath tub with a wooden surround and panel. It was amazing and we desperately wanted to keep it.

The bath proved to be beyond resurrection but we carefully kept the panel. I stripped and treated it and eventually it was used in one of the hotel bedrooms. The panel had to be made a little shorter as the original bath was much bigger than our modern ones. Martin made a new surround. We had to find a really nice hardwood and he eventually used Douglas fir the same as the bar. We had some left over

Old bath in derelict wing

Bath after treatment and new top

and he used it to make me a really big chopping board which we eventually used for a cheese board in the restaurant.

Because we would now be having guests, we had to make sure that the septic tanks and drainage were adequate.

Tom, our neighbour came with his digger and set to work in the biggest walled garden. When finished the two chambers were absolutely enormous, big enough to hold a double decker bus. We reckoned it could accommodate the whole of Reynoldston.

It seemed as though the garden was a mass of holes, ditches and drains and I thought it would never recover to grow vegetables again – but it did.

Chapter Five

Since the Planning Notice had been on the gate, so many of the local people showed their approval and indeed, some even expressed genuine excitement at the idea. The majority, however, thought us crazy and said we would never get people to travel out here.

I was having the occasional nightmare but generally, at this stage, keeping my panic at bay!

I don't know whether John had won me over or whether I had just been worn down. The hotel idea did appeal but I could also see the reality of it all and didn't want to let myself in for all the commitment.

We were spending a great deal of money – five wages and materials. A loan from the Welsh Development Agency was our best bet. We applied and went with our plan, for a preliminary interview.

They wanted to know how many staff we would employ – waitresses, cleaners, chamber maids, etc. This started me panicking again as I could feel the control taken from my hands. How could we commit ourselves to such fine details when Fairyhill was still more or less a ruin! I couldn't think of waitresses yet!

Our plan at this time was to have residents in eleven bedrooms and then perhaps take bookings from any outsiders who might like to eat. I would be in the kitchen and would do a different menu every night; choice of two starters, set main course, dessert and cheese with a glass of suitable wine provided to accompany each course. A set meal and wine. No choice. No one had the nerve to do that!

The idea really appealed to us. To walk into a restaurant and not have to make a decision. As you do when going to a friend's for dinner. Maybe I could even get some friends to take turns cooking their favourite meal? Maggi Tuesdays, Joanna Fridays, etc. We thought we'd hit a winner. John would be 'out front' and would be a strong enough personality to persuade people that this was what they wanted! We were sure it would work.

We were very concerned about the stream. In parts it could hardly be seen because of the undergrowth and fallen trees and branches. It would be a mammoth task and John was worried as to how he could tackle it. As far as he could see he would need at least a crane and a JCB. The latter was on my birthday list!

Anyway, we were to have a lucky break. I was washing down some shutters in the courtyard one afternoon when a man approached asking for the owner (no one ever believed I was the owner as I always looked like a tramp). He said he was from the River Board and asked if they could have permission to come onto our land to clean out the river. I called John and asked for the question to be repeated. We were so thrilled and couldn't believe that we were having all this help – unasked!

The men said they had never had such a reception. Sometimes people resented the intrusion. It took four of them three weeks with heavy machinery to clear it, but we were so grateful. They piled up all the dead trees in the orchard ready for John to cut up into logs.

Staff "patio"

Staff "patio"

We had some friends staying with us from Yorkshire. Actually, it was Guinevere's sister, Stephanie and her husband Christopher, and we all worked outside.

We tried to hack our way around the back of the billiard room to make a path into the walled garden. The men spent most of the time with chain saws edging their way slowly through. Chris, was like someone possessed cutting through everything in his path and I arrived in the nick of time to save what proved to be a wonderful red may tree. Indeed, in years to come it blossomed into quite a show piece and one of the best sights in the grounds. It was to be the background to many a wedding photograph.

We cleared the whole area behind the billiard room which had been filled with overgrown rhododendrons, some of which reached the roof. Having removed all this rubbish by means of the biggest bonfire yet, it revealed to us an opening between the billiard room and the west wing and a door which turned out to lead into the cellar. A second doorway led to a storeroom but we could get to these only by digging down through accumulated sediment and rubbish at least three feet thick. We just kept going until we came to a proper paved floor, scrabbling across two steps. There was yet another doorway which was to lead into the gunroom and kitchen.

It took us a long time to worm our way into the cellar which was directly under the billiard room. We inched our way through the rubbish and 'emilies' with hand torches and made out the old wine bins and rusty racks. We groped into the first bin and our hands came across bottles. They were heavy and felt very interesting. We grabbed a few and very carefully carried them out to the daylight. They were probably fine wines of an ancient vintage. Claret perhaps or even port? We anticipated a visit to Sotheby's as we brushed off the dust. What did we find? Distilled water! Dozens of bottles. Probably used for the batteries before the time of the generator.

In time, this cellar was put to its proper use again, but first, the ceiling, which was the floor of the billiard room, had to be stripped out and burnt as it was so rotten. Every inch of wall cleaned off, sprayed against dry rot and prepared for renewal.

We had already ordered the billiard table so that spurred us on!

After clearance and renovation

House with ponies

Two black sheep had found their way into the parkland and were there for weeks, grazing most contentedly. A ewe and her lamb. One day, a flock of sheep arrived and our little lamb was so excited to see them. She frisked and jumped around and tried to join them. They appeared terrified and as soon as she got near, they ran for their lives. Poor thing. Perhaps they thought she was a dog as she was black. Anyway, they would have nothing to do with her and she eventually gave up.

This was the start of sheep coming in to Fairyhill. The gates had always been closed in the past but now there was nothing to keep them out. We rather liked to see them grazing on the lawn and they did keep the grass down and the paths open.

They were soon to be followed by the wild ponies and this we really enjoyed. They were to continue coming in over the years to give great pleasure to us and our residents. We deliberately didn't plant flowers or many shrubs. We preferred the animals if we had to chose. We made up by having lots of hanging baskets that the sheep couldn't reach.

There must have been a lot of bats in residence in the end room of the east wing. The floor was covered with droppings. We did see a solitary bat hanging there one day but she could never have done all that on her own.

John had to go up into the roof space above these rooms one day to inspect a water tank. He shone his torch around and shouted down – "It's absolutely full of emilies!"

The bats continued to roost in this wing and also in the main roof space. It was, and still is one of the largest roosts in Gower, having no less than seven different species at the last count in 1991. We had a problem for a few years in as much as the bats would come in through any window on the east side that was left open. They had always done it. We had to tell people to keep their windows shut!

Because of the bats, we had to chose the right time to put six large water storage tanks into the roof.

We used spring water and had to lay a new alkathene pipe to replace the lead pipe, half a mile from the spring to the house. Once again, it was Tom who did this for us. The spring was near to the one that fed Burry Cottage garden and by this time John was very familiar with it and found his way there easily. The water came from under the hill into a large reservoir and could only be stopped coming through the pipe by inserting a bung.

Tom dug the new trench all the way to Fairyhill. He then had to get under the road and across the courtyard. We had the foresight to branch off supply pipes to the Coach House, Stable and farmyard.

Because the source of our water was high up on Cefn Bryn and travelled downhill to us, the pressure was enormous and there was no difficulty in reaching the storage tanks in the roof. We thought ourselves really lucky to have this water. We had it tested of course, and it passed with flying colours. When we first opened the restaurant the Public Health were to visit us every three months to test that it was alright but gradually, the visits became less frequent.

The kitchen area in the east wing was a very daunting task. We gutted it and made the two rooms and passageway into one huge room. We would have the cooking area up one end and then the dresser and big farmhouse table at the bottom end.

The earthed floor old kitchen was beyond this room. We found an enormous old porcelain sink which we eventually put out there and this was invaluable for washing up large pans, etc. This room was to house the laundry machines, linen and dish and glass-washers.

Leading off the kitchen was the lamp and gun room which was to house all the dry stores, crockery and glasses.

Under the rubble in the gun room we found an enormous wooden cupboard which I repaired, stripped and sealed. It turned out to be the housekeeper's original linen cupboard so we took it out to the old kitchen and continued to use it as a linen cupboard.

Mrs. Beynon, who lives in Reynoldston and was housekeeper to Mr. Harris back in the 1940's was thrilled to see it on a later visit to us.

Past the lamp room was the dairy and pantry which we knocked together to form a larger room. The beam we used to support this ceiling was an old tree that John pulled up from the woods and it looked magnificent. This room we furnished as a sitting room and this is where we were to live when we initially moved in. We had made one window into a door which now led out onto a large patio behind the billiard room. This little sitting room was later to be used as a very cosy staffroom.

Having already spent a year working on Fairyhill, we sold Burry Cottage. The people who bought it assured us that they liked garden-

Martin, John and Roddy with beam for staff room ceiling

ing – which was just as well. John explained the garden water system and how he had got it all working and said he would help them to fix it should it ever stop again.

We moved down to Fairyhill the same way we had moved from Mumbles – a room at a time. No van this time but just the Land Rover and trailer. I can thoroughly recommend it. No packing cases or removal men. We made about six trips with me in the trailer hanging onto whatever we were taking at the time.

Most of our furniture was stored in the drawing and dining rooms which had been more or less completed and we, as I said, lived in the staff room. We had a woodstove there and it was warm and attractive.

Although we had electricity and a microwave, we had no cooking stove so barbecued most of our main meals. It's amazing what can be done with a spit on a small cheap barbecue. Whole chickens, shoulder or leg of lamb in addition to steaks. All fish and potatoes we wrapped in foil and put in the dying embers of the endless bonfires.

After the death of Lil and Nellie, we had two more kittens in Burry Cottage – Winni and Peg. Poor Peg had been run over just like little Nell so now we were left with Winni the Purr. We were worried about her moving down to Fairyhill and left her till last. We took her out of her basket and let her into our little sitting room. I didn't want her to go outside, but she jumped onto the window sill and it was obvious that she wanted to explore. I said to John, "Just take her as far as the front lawn."

She has always been inquisitive and this would not do. We had to let her go. She went for a couple of hours and then arrived back to look at us through the window. What a relief!

That night, we took her up to bed with us to the room directly above at the top of the back stairs. I wanted to keep her in there as most of the floor boards were up on the first floor landing for the plumbers and electricians. I visualised her being lost under the floors and never getting out. She insisted on going and must have explored all of the thirty plus rooms. She was gone for hours and I eventually fell asleep. When we woke in the morning, there she was, safe and sound, curled up on our bed. What a clever cat!

Now that we were to be an hotel, we contacted the Fire Department and had a visit from the Fire Prevention Officer. They are very strict on safety and we had to do quite a lot of things that we would have preferred not to.

Where I had planned a wide open archway in the hall to match up with the alcoves, he insisted we had fire doors. He was a very sympathetic man who had done a lot of renovating himself and appreciated what we were trying to do. I couldn't bear the thought of conventional fire doors which would be virtually the first thing to be seen on entering through the front door.

He eventually agreed to my idea of using two of our old doors, removing the panels and replacing them with fireproof glass. I was very grateful to him. However, I couldn't get away with the bedroom doors and had to stick some awful fireproof material over my lovely stripped wood. I'm sure that the doors were so thick that they would have taken days to burn through.

We also had to build a wall at the top of the stairs which spoilt a very pretty landing.

We managed to work out most things very amicably and parted the best of friends.

Martha Gatwick helping herself as usual

Our chickens had settled in very well. They had two large hen houses and the run of the walled garden. This wasn't enough for Martha Gatwick who roamed freely around the front lawn, parkland and inside the house at any chance she could get. She was an opportunist and any food lying around was fair game.

One day, I had left a bowl of strawberries on the kitchen table. I approached from one end of the kitchen as Martha Gatwick strolled through the back door. She spotted the strawberries and, wings back, neck outstretched she half ran, half flew and just beat me to it. By the time I managed to scoop the bowl away, her beak, like a pneumatic drill, had pierced at least half a dozen!

She was an amazing bird. People calling in would shout out, "There's a chicken in the hall!"

I made elderflower champagne every summer and was sampling the first bottle. I stretched myself out on a sunbed for half an hour's rest and took my first sip. It was lovely, but far too gassy to drink so I decided to leave it for ten minutes to calm down. After the due time, I reached down to pick up my glass, which was on the floor, and was surprised to see that it was half empty.

Martha Gatwick was walking slowly down the lawn alternately opening her beak wide and stretching out her neck. She was obviously full of wind and I thought that was the end of her. She came right after a while but she wasn't put off – gin and tonic, whisky – she only had to see a glass and would run at speed to land on any unsuspecting lap. Very unnerving for those who weren't prepared. When we ate outdoors we had to send her into her own garden first!

It just goes to show how intelligent she was, given plenty of freedom. What a different life our chickens had compared to the poor battery hens. Our egg yolks were orange from the varied diet they had, not pale yellow. Anyone digging the garden would be surrounded by chickens waiting for worms.

Hugh, from Stackpole Mill, next door had joined the work force. He said he could use a blow lamp so I put him to burn off the old paint on the fan light over the billiard room which Frank had removed. He seemed to finish this very quickly and when I looked, all the wood was badly scorched. When I pointed it out to him he proceeded to tell me that it wasn't possible to burn off paint without damaging the wood! Luckily this window was to be repainted as it was well beyond anything else. While Frank was able to remove these windows from the roof of the billiard room, that still left the frames in situ. I had to go up onto the roof, climbing precariously from the gully at the side of the gun room, and cling on to the window frame in order to clean off the remaining paint. I couldn't use the blow lamp as I didn't have enough hands! I was definitely not happy and the only way I could do it was by tying a large leather strap around my waist and the window so now I couldn't fall off the roof. To get at the inside, Frank erected scaffolding in the billiard room with a plank stretched the length of it. I don't like heights and this was the only job I failed to do. As I walked along this plank it 'twanged' so John had to finish it off for me.

There was a very pretty staircase in the hall which turned gently towards the top. Martin discovered it had been made in two parts and was able to remove it totally. We needed to do this to treat the dry rot underneath and the whole of the outside wall.

I dismantled the banister rail which had been deeply scratched while the Philpotts were moving out, and removed all the spindles for stripping. Whilst doing this I was distressed to discover that three of the spindles were not wood at all but made of iron. This was probably for extra support at strategic points. I was very much afraid that I would have to paint the whole staircase. Anyway, I pressed on and eventually, having completed the stripping, dying and sealing, managed to camouflage the iron spindles by painting them the right colour brown and varnishing. They were never spotted unless pointed out and I was quite proud of that achievement.

I can't imagine how many gas refills I had for my trusty blowlamp or how many sheets of sandpaper I used. I remember that my finger tips were sometimes quite smooth with little spots of blood showing through. I think I had worn my finer prints away. I often wondered whether I would ever again have lovely long polished finger nails!

I always felt a thrill starting on a really bad piece of wood when the flame of my burner did its job and my scraper pulled down cleanly and instantly revealed the wood grain. It amazed me that the smell of resin in the pitch pine was so strong and fresh. I would always, in my head, talk to it and welcome it to a new lease of life – good for another few hundred years now!

Chapter Six

I had always loved the idea of having a goat and I thought this would be a perfect place. Plenty of room to wander about and goodness knows, there was more than enough to eat.

I knew a wonderful lady called 'Brookie'. Her real name was Ann Brookes, affectionately called 'the goat guru of Gower'. To visit her home was, for me, to step into an animal paradise. Lots of goats, of course, housed in deep litter pens, each with the friend of its preference and their respective kids. All free to roam during the day but with shelter whenever needed.

Stables were next to the goat house forming an L shaped block – all beautifully kept and spotlessly clean. The goat milking parlour sparkled from the stainless steel everywhere. Chickens and fowls of all kinds seemed to wander at will and on entering the kitchen one would be met by dogs, cats and three rabbits together with any other animal that needed attention. This was a home where animals came first. In fact, Brookie is an acknowledged authority on homoeopathic treatment for animals and well-respected throughout the country. In addition to this, she is a very original character and I loved my visits there. She wasn't pleased to see everyone so I was quite flattered that I was always welcome.

I told her that I would like a goat and she asked me my reasons. I said I had always loved them and also needed one to eat the grass and everything else. Well, it wasn't going to be that easy. She insisted on visiting first to see the goat house and where it would be.

I spent a whole day scrubbing out and disinfecting one of the chicken houses and by the time she came it was sparkling. We had to remove the glass from the window and make a canopy over it to keep out the rain but still let in the air. Hay and straw went onto the floor and it had to be cleaned out every day!

When she eventually brought Petal, she was accompanied by Petal's daughter, Primula. All Brookie's goats had names beginning with the letter 'P'. "I couldn't possibly separate them, and you have so much space."

I told her my plan of letting them graze in the park but this was no good. "They'll wander off in no time, and rhododendrons are poisonous." When I suggested that I might tether them, she went very quiet, then said, "My goats are NEVER tethered!"

Oh dear, I'd really lost my stripes now, and quickly did all I could to reassure her, muttering that I hadn't thought and, of course, she was quite right and naturally, I wouldn't dream of tethering them.

This wasn't really what I had in mind at all. I loved them dearly and they were great characters. We kept them enclosed in the big walled garden which I could get to through the scullery, which was now full of hay. The scullery had a stable door and was the favourite place for Petal and Primula. They would stand outside on hind legs with front hooves over the edge of the bottom door, head and shoulders peering over the top. A very pretty picture. They kept calling until someone came to give them a rub and a chat. If the door should be left open, of course, they were in. Things were much more interesting inside!

I was true to Brookie and every day would put on my wellies and rubber gloves, clean out the goat house, change the bedding and supply fresh sweet 'organic' hay which cost me a fortune. They wouldn't eat what wasn't fresh and naturally, they never touched our weeds!

I think it was about this time that we decided we needed to know something about kitchen equipment. What was available and how it worked. We thought the best way to go about things would be to enrol for a gentle catering course in the local College of Further Education.

We duly enrolled for a one-day-a-week course held every Tuesday. Well, it appeared that we had ourselves involved in a production kitchen – serious stuff. It meant that we had to turn up in chef's whites, trousers and hat! A few books and a complete set of knives each were also required.

Everyone worked in pairs and the meal produced at the end of the morning was served to the public in a training restaurant adjoining the kitchen This was far more advanced than we had anticipated. I drew the short straw in the partnership stakes and had John for the whole course!

Petal and Primula at the scullery door

The rest of the class consisted of youngsters, most of whom were already working in restaurants and who were there for day release for their qualifications. The general age was between seventeen and twenty. We upped the average considerably being well over twice their age and in John's case, nearly three times!

We took everything very seriously and worked hard. We all made bread first thing on arrival. Then some weeks were on starters and sometimes on main courses or desserts. I seemed to spend a lot of time washing up as I can't work in a mess. It was fatal to stay near the sink as everyone seemed to appear with their dirty dishes. I soon wised up to that.

It was strange being with people so much younger. I suppose it was still like school to them and some tried to do as little as possible, whereas we were desperate to learn as much as we could. I think Kim, our tutor, was quite bemused.

One of the first things to happen on arrival at nine o'clock was that all the ovens and grills were switched full on. This was too much for John. He dug me in the ribs and said "Look at that – no wonder our rates are so high. Switch them off, Midge!"

We had lots of giggles and although John did his best, and very well considering he knew nothing about cooking, I ended up doing a lot more than my fair share, including hiding his mistakes!

I don't know whether we gained much useful knowledge that we really used, but it was an experience.

The main factor to arise out of this episode was to change the course of Fairyhill.

We asked Kim, our tutor, if he would be kind enough to visit us at Fairyhill to advise us on kitchen equipment and where to situate various things. He said he would be delighted and could come the following Saturday morning. This he did but telephoned beforehand to ask if he could bring a friend. They both arrived and we duly gave them the grand tour – house and grounds. This took ages but they both seemed so enchanted with everything that the time flew by. We had some lunch and spent a pleasant afternoon.

Kate, Kim's friend, eventually said she had to go as she was cooking that evening. She was working at a restaurant in Mumbles called 'The Old School House'. She was mostly managing but sometimes filled in cooking. She had never been trained formally as a chef but was a fanatical foodie and a brilliant cook. We liked her tremendously.

In fact, that evening, we decided to visit the Old School House and maybe we could have a look at the kitchen. This turned out to be absolutely tiny. Ours was ten times bigger!

Kate had heard that we were booked in to the restaurant and when we had finished our meal, which we enjoyed immensely, she came out to see us and we all had a drink.

She said she hadn't been able to get Fairyhill out of her mind, it was so beautiful. She also said that if we wanted a chef that she would give anything to work there. I told her my plan for 'dinner party nights' and that we were keeping things low key and hadn't planned for a chef. We said we'd think about it.

I had been suffering from headaches – very unlike me, and when

John visited an osteopath for an injured shoulder, I went with him. My neck was stiff and he told me I was very tense, and should relax more. As far as I was concerned, I was enjoying every minute of every day and loving my hard but satisfying labours.

After our day with Kate we discussed her proposition and thought long and hard. If we had to find all the extra money for a chef and extra staff we would have to change our ideas. Maybe do weddings and lunches. Did we want this? Well, we decided we would give Kate a try. I telephoned her and told her the news. This was about November 1984 which gave her four months before we needed her so she could give her employers plenty of notice.

Immediately this decision had been taken, my headaches left me so I suppose it must have been tension. I knew that Kate would relieve me of a lot of decisions and she also had the knowledge and experience of how to stock up on equipment and the thousand and one other things we would need.

Needless to say, she was thrilled when I spoke to her and couldn't wait for the luxury of such a huge kitchen. I remember her saying "I think I can make a name for myself at Fairyhill, Midgie."

Well, that was a huge step to take and now I really felt as though we had changed from our home being a guest house to it becoming an hotel and restaurant.

From the time we had started on the renovations there was tremendous interest in what we were doing. Fairyhill had always held a fascination for locals and everyone was itching to see what was going on. In addition to this was the fact that John was very well-known in and around Swansea and people knew that whatever he was doing, would be done properly.

Kate, who was forever popping in, was hoping to have a 'Grand Opening' party and had a list of complimentary guests. We pointed out that there were dozens of people itching to come so why not let them pay!

Chapter Seven

We were being plagued by laundries offering their services. We had already agreed to lease launderette machines so that we could be totally self-sufficient. Jennifer, a friend of mine, who at that time ran a small hotel in Sketty, introduced us to a company which as an inducement to one taking the largest machines, offered us free towels, table-cloths of our choice, napkins, sheets and pillowcases. Dozens of everything. I thought it an amazing offer and it clinched the deal.

These machines proved to be invaluable over the years and one of the best decisions ever taken. They hardly ever stopped working and we were never short of clean linen. Nothing had to be ironed if removed from the dryer immediately as all creases were smoothed out in the machine. They also enabled us to do all guests' laundry which I did free of charge if I liked them! We could also dry out rain-drenched clothing in a very short time.

One morning we found our black sheep lying in the Coach House. She had died during the night and her lamb was asleep next to her. We had a job to get her away from the mother although by now she was fully grown. It was very sad and I took her down to the park. We called her 'Orphan Annie' and she stayed in the grounds for well over a year. I don't know what happened to her eventually. Perhaps she was rounded up with another flock. Company at last! She had a very lonely life.

We managed to find some wonderful hand-painted wash-basins and lavatories. Italian, and frighteningly expensive but once seen, nothing else would do. We splashed out on four sets of these. Three of our biggest rooms would have them with one set in the Coach House We also had a smaller set for the Ladies' and Gent's toilets.

We found it difficult to stick to a budget as neither of us could resist the quality and Italian design. We were also to excel ourselves with the carpets!

We could balance the cost of these against what we saved on some of the curtains.

When we had moved from Mumbles, we had taken our sitting room and dining room curtains. As the windows there had been so vast, I was able to shorten them for Burry Cottage.

I don't think I have mentioned that I have this disease inherited from my mother. I NEVER throw anything away! Because of this, it's imperative that we always move to larger houses.

I knew that I could use these curtains yet again by replacing the material I had cut off and stored away and so save us a great deal of money. The dining room curtains would fit the Billiard Room and the sitting room curtains could be made to fit the Dining Room.

I really do get enormous satisfaction from this. Perhaps it's something to do with being a war baby and brought up during rationing!

Friends and acquaintances would always call (especially on weekends) to see how we were getting on. My mother would usually come, having made Welsh cakes that we could offer with a cup of tea. This was all very nice but on a 'bad' day we could be held up for hours.

John would usually escort these visitors around the house, explaining what we had done and all about our plans. On entering the room where I was working with my blow lamp one day, I was amused to hear him telling them, "Oh yes, Midge is the best stripper in Gower!"

Everyone expected a 'tour' and with about thirty rooms this could take a considerable time. If the grounds became involved, it could be hours. Sometimes, total strangers would drive in for a look, and we didn't have a sign up at this stage. Let's hope they continue to drive in when we are open!

Between all the physical work of decorating we now had to get cracking to find carpets. I always think these are the most important part of house furnishing and are the one item on which we have never skimped.

People would usually make the comment – specially women when they saw me in my work clothes with blow lamp or paint brush –

that I must be looking forward to the exciting bit of buying furnishings. Totally wrong. I found it exhausting. I was more content to stay working with the builders and having to leave them to search for carpets was a bind.

Making it more difficult was the fact that I usually have a picture in my head of what I'm after. Pattern, but with colours to fit in with furniture and things we already have and, colours that would look good with all my lovely wood.

It was imperative that we found the carpet now as it could take months to deliver.

We eventually found what we wanted – we both loved them – about double the price we had intended to pay, but once seen, nothing else was going to do. Super Kershan Wilton in the most beautiful colours.

One was going to start in the front door and continue to hall, office, bar, passageways, up the stairs and right through the first floor landings.

An equally beautiful subdued pattern for the drawing room which would blend with our green leather furniture and, indeed anything else we chose to put in there.

For the dining room, again Super Kershan in the most wonderful olive green with a small traditional pattern. My mustard velvet curtains would be good with it. The ceilings and frieze would be painted the same colour as the curtains. The chairs we had found for the dining room would have their seats covered in the same olive green leather. It was a great relief to have the carpets sorted out and there would only be about a month for the order to be delivered. A huge weight off my mind.

For the Billiard Room we chose another pattern which matched extremely well with our old Sanderson curtains. The billiard table was already on order and we had found some wooden bench seats which had been thrown out of an old pub in Swansea. We could put these around two of the walls each side of the woodstove. Things were really moving now!

Whilst they were in the region of the Coach House the builders also put a new roof on the stable. I knew that sometime in the future

Midge and John outside original stable

New roof to stable. New "stall" gates in position

Stable as it is now

we would turn this into a house. I wanted arches and a gallery some-where but, in the meantime, with its new roof, we could use it as a wood store and home for the tractor.

Outside the stable, when we had cleared away lots of old bushes, we unearthed what looked like cobbles. We were excited and I spent days on my hands and knees uncovering the whole area. We also found an old ha'penny worn quite smooth which we kept for luck. John still carries it with him at all times. I think of the hours spent on the cobbles and years later we had to dig them up to lower the ground level!

Inside the stable were two enormous stall partitions and Mark had the brilliant idea of using them for gates at the driveway entrance between the Stable and the Coach House. They could never be closed but then we needed them to be open at all times. We man-aged to do it but it took six men to lift one of them. I don't know what they must have weighed.

The area at the back between the main house, Bothey house, Stable and Coach house I had envisaged as a courtyard with trees and shrubs and lots of pots and paved areas. Of course, once we had de-cided to be an hotel we realised that we would need as much parking space as possible. It was a problem to know how to cover this area. As far as I could see, there was only tarmac, paving or gravel. The first was awful, the second too expensive which only left gravel. To blend in with the overall colouring of the Gower stonework, we decided on the more golden colour of Cotswold chippings. It proved very effective but labour intensive to keep free from weeds and fallen twigs and leaves.

We had some brochures printed with a lovely photograph of the house through the trees and ponies on the grass. Inside was a picture of the hall with Celyn sitting in front of the open woodstove. It was very unpretentious and just what we wanted.

John could enjoy himself now 'selling' Fairyhill. He went to all the large multinationals in and around Swansea telling them what a tranquil haven of peace there was soon to be for their harassed and work-worn businessmen and visitors. This was John's forte. I was the worker and he was the entrepreneur. He liked the organising and marketing side of things. I didn't, so we were a perfect team.

We were aiming at the business market rather than holiday makers which was indeed what we succeeded in attracting initially.

Courtyard area

We wanted our signs to look traditional and had them made from varnished wood with gold lettering 'Fairyhill Country House Hotel and Restaurant'. We thought they looked perfect. We had one outside each gate and one at the crossroads on our wall. At the Stembridge end of the lane we asked Mathias Taylor, a local farmer who owned the wall if we could have permission to affix our sign there, and he agreed. He was a strange man who drove around the lanes at fifteen miles an hour holding everybody up. He was also renting the old Fairyhill home farm opposite.

We had a fifth swinging sign in black and gold on the main South Gower road for which we paid an annual rent to the Penrice Estate.

We both think that signs are important and we wanted the style to portray the sort of establishment we were running – couth!

Incidentally, we had a visit from someone in the City Council telling us we had to change these wooden signs for white plastic! No chance. We totally ignored that and heard no more about it.

Courtyard after clearing

Clearing cobbles outside stable

Guinevere, who you will remember is Celyn's fairy godmother, telephoned to ask if we had a short term job for Dominic, her son, who was then about nineteen and saving for a trip to Australia. He said he would do anything so we agreed and he came every morning and worked with the builders. Dobs pitched into anything that was offered and as time went on even helped with washing up and 'waitressing'. He is a super chap and gets on with everyone, young or old. He was with us for most of the summer and really enjoyed himself. He wanted to try his hand at everything.

By the time we opened the following April (1985) we would have only two bedrooms on the first floor and the four attic rooms. We were still working on the remaining five rooms.

At least we could start slowly with the residential side and concentrate mainly on the restaurant. I was still very wary.

Kate arrived with us a lot sooner than anticipated. She left her old job soon after Christmas. She was probably so excited about Fairyhill and couldn't stop talking about it which wouldn't go down very well with her employers.

She started with us about February 1985 and we were quite glad of the extra time as there was a lot to do ordering crockery, cutlery, glasses and all the dozens of pieces of equipment. She was able to spend time in London investigating various suppliers and generally planning what to put where. She was enjoying herself. She even did some sanding down of doors for me, but I decided she should stick to cooking!

Expenses were rising by the day. Kate would need someone full time with her in the kitchen and also extra part-time assistance. We hadn't bargained for this. Waitresses and cleaners had to be vetted but Kate took all this responsibility from me which left me free to continue with my decorating, as time was pressing on.

She seemed to know so many people. I suppose this was because she had worked in lots of different places and all catering staff seem to move around.

We were to start with two youngsters helping her in the kitchen. Alison who lived in Llangennith and Claire from Mumbles. They would both also wait at table so could fill in wherever needed most.

It seemed that everyone wanted to work at Fairyhill and we were inundated with enquiries. We still had Joyce, of course, who had followed us down from Burry Cottage. She had been cleaning around the builders' mess since we moved in. I don't think we ever did advertise for staff the word just seemed to travel round.

Quite unintentionally it turned out that we were all female. Nothing to do with feminism, but as it was to prove so successful over the years, we never actively sought men in our midst!

We were getting perilously close to opening. This was March and we were opening mid April 1985.

Reps came in an unending stream selling everything imaginable, to hinder me.

I had long since decided that I would be using lace table-cloths over coloured linen undercloths. Also, I would have large unstarched linen napkins. Another of my 'hates' had always been stiff, unwieldy napkins. Like wiping the mouth with a sheet of cardboard!

Midge and mum in drawing room

Drawing room with 'monstrosity' on right

All these could be laundered daily at Fairyhill together with all sheets, pillowcases, towels and tea-towels. The only things that went to the laundry were chefs' whites, aprons and hats. Eventually, we were to stop sending these as I was forever sewing on buttons and apron strings.

Something I found extraordinary was the fact that we were frequently told that we were inexperienced and shouldn't do things this way or that. We were almost scorned. It seemed that hotels had certain ways of doing things and how dare we deviate. It was earth-shattering that we should have lace cloths and not linen like everyone else.

The hot air hand dryer reps assured me that I couldn't put nice towels in the cloakrooms as they would be stolen!

The fruit machine people were the worst. They couldn't believe that we could refuse the large profits their machines would generate.

It was our hotel and we could do it any way we liked!

The worst was done in the east wing. The men had almost finished so it was down to me with the decorating. They could gain any access required via the fire escape which meant we could have the carpets laid in the rest of the house.

We had many trips in search of beds, curtains and a hundred other things. There was nothing stereotyped about the rooms. They were all shapes and sizes – each one with its own identity. This was mainly because we hadn't bought anything commercially. We had made a trip to the Hotel and Catering Exhibition but hadn't really been tempted to buy anything. Anyway, it was all so expensive and it must be borne in mind that we were a very small business in a personal environment.

We did splash out on soaps and shampoos. These were Roger & Gallet and I had always liked them. We also ordered a variety of 'Taylors' teas to put in all our bedrooms.

We had numbered the bedrooms with three figures which would double as the telephone number. This made life easier for everyone. The first floor would be 211 to 217 and the second floor would be 221 to 224. In years to come the Coach House would be 230 the Stable 240/1, the Barn 250/1 and the farm buildings 260 etc.

Suddenly, it was looking more like home. Pugh's in Llanelli had made the curtains for the office, hall, bar, drawing room and our two best bedrooms. I was making all the others.

It seemed to me unbelievable that now we had the carpets down, our plumbing seemed to crack up. I had told Don, our plumber, to make certain everything was tested and in working order beforehand. After that I don't think a day went by that I didn't go into a room to find water dripping through a ceiling. I was spending a great deal of time patrolling and mopping. The worst was in the main hall when, one morning, John found the floor totally covered with water. This, on our wonderful new carpet – really, it was almost too much to bear.

I was upset and extremely irate and could have strangled Don when he said, "Don't keep calling them leaks, Midge – they are not leaks". "Really Don, then what is the water coming through the ceiling?" "Faulty joints." I couldn't believe it. It was the most distressing time.

John was still working hard in the grounds and, as nearly two years had been spent on them his efforts were being rewarded. We had planted some shrubs outside the Conservatory which we brought from Burry Cottage and a few rhododendrons further down amongst the trees.

We had planted literally hundreds of young trees all through the grounds and orchard. This was done with the help of the Environmental Department. I would think that probably half of those planted survived but it was to be ten years before they began to gain any decent growth, being all broad leafed. Now they look really good and we are proud to have done it. They are replacing the original trees that are coming to the end of their lives. Needless to say these are an endless supply of fuel for our four wood burning stoves.

We had decided not to create any sort of garden – no flowers apart from hanging baskets. We had enjoyed Burry Cottage but its three acres of intensive care ruled our lives, even with two gardeners and we were determined not to make any more work than necessary. Anyway, the sheep and ponies wandered in and out at leisure and any flowers had to be well above grazing level. We concentrated on making the paths and parkland attractive.

When John wants to buy anything really expensive – I get it for a present, as a joke of course. I had a tractor for my birthday and a log splitter for Christmas. These had now been moved from the stable into a specially built shed in the big walled garden. The shed is mainly for our logs which have to be cut and stored for two years before using, so at least one day a week was set aside for cutting and splitting them – summer and winter. We loved our woodstoves so much we never minded this effort.

Well, now the carpets were down and the ground floor was ready. The tables and chairs were in the dining room and we had three tables in the conservatory, all able to seat four people. Our pictures and ornaments didn't go far in decorating the walls and we would have to spend yet more precious time searching for bits and pieces. This would have to wait as every minute of the working day was taken up fighting the clock.

I thought I was working quite hard. It was nothing compared to what was to come!

Now everything was happening. China, cutlery, glasses, kitchen equipment and a hundred bits and pieces were arriving daily.

We had quite a problem finding the china. We had wanted to buy British, i.e. Wedgewood or Doulton but were told there would be anything up to six months delivery. Eventually, we settled on Rosenthal which was one of Germany's best. It was more expensive but at least we could have it without delay. Ironically, the Germans have a six month delivery date on this themselves but can get our Wedgewood or Royal Doulton quickly!

Our on-site laundry was installed and we had bought a second hand dishwasher and stainless steel sink and drainer which was next to our lovely big porcelain sink. We were now ready to function on a low scale.

I found it very strange that people were just walking into the front hall and wandering around and had to stop myself being 'prickly'. As far as I was concerned this was my home and it was unnerving to bump into total strangers. I had to remind myself that there was a sign outside saying 'Hotel and Restaurant' but it was to take time for me to come to terms with this.

One afternoon I was interviewing someone in the drawing room when Kate appeared around the door gesturing frantically. I excused myself and walked down to her. She was babbling something I couldn't understand but could sense the urgency. She repeated it more slowly – "Quick, the Environmental Health Inspector is in the hall. I'll stall her. You go through and get the cat off the greaseproof paper and shoo that bloody chicken out of the kitchen." We kept a pile of greaseproof paper on a low shelf and Winni loved to curl up on this. We always removed the top sheet.

We also had to keep the scullery door closed as this was full of the goats' hay. Incidentally, we thereafter had an excellent hygiene record and after all, we were not yet open!

We had to think about a receptionist and general secretary. Secretarial work was what I had always done but I didn't want to get involved in that side of things. There was so much else to worry about.

We sought out Val who had been John's secretary in the Kingsway shop. The three of us had done all the buying together. We had lost touch in recent years but had heard that she was not working. John contacted her and she was delighted at the thought of working with us again.

Val was and is very smart and fashion conscious in addition to being extremely meticulous and honest and would be a big asset to us. Her hours were to be half past seven in the morning until half past three in the afternoon Mondays to Fridays and she was to see to all the paper work, accounts and wages.

Chapter Eight

As I said, we were not having an opening party. We wanted to slip into things slowly. Kate said she would like to start with a Sunday lunch with her parents and some friends from the Yacht Club – about twenty people in all. This sounded sensible and, more to the point manageable as it was so new to us. John was excited and I was terrified!

They were due to arrive at half past midday and I dashed around all morning, fussing over tables, flowers and waitresses. I eventually went upstairs to change to be down in the hall ready to welcome them when they arrived.

Unbeknown to me, they had arrived about ten minutes early and as I came down the stairs and approached the bar I could hear this chatter and I completely lost my nerve. I turned around and went straight back upstairs to the bedroom with Celyn close on my heels. I took a deep breath and tried again – same thing. I just couldn't bring myself to walk into a room full of strangers. Intruders in my home! I shook and I cried. Celyn stayed with me all the time and was a comfort. I was up there for hours. Eventually, after half a dozen cigarettes I gave myself a good talking to and Celyn and I walked down together.

By this time, of course, lunch was finished and everyone was back in the bar or drawing room. Nothing was mentioned and I chatted to everyone and was alright. In retrospect, I would have been fine had I been in position in the hall when they arrived. It's a terrible thing to lose one's nerve. It had happened to me once before, trying to drop anchor in Ilfracombe harbour – but that's another story!

We were opening the following Thursday night and were fully booked. Twelve in the conservatory and eighteen in the dining room. Most of these people were locals who had promised to be critical and give us an honest opinion of the food and general atmosphere.

I thought the rooms looked lovely. Chairs matching carpet. Mustard colour linen cloths showing through the lace and the same colour napkins, curtains and candles. The frieze and ceiling were also that colour, a cross between mustard and old gold. We used our own brass candlesticks and I had done pretty flowers for each table.

We had a super antique cupboard against the wall on which we had the desserts, fruit and a cheeseboard. The lighting was nice from half a dozen lamps around the room.

We had three waitresses that first night. Ann and Beryl who had worked with Kate before and were to stay with us for many years, and a young girl called Georgina who lived locally.

Kate was in the kitchen of course, with Alison and Claire ready for action.

John was in the bar with Shirley, Kate's father and her mother Doreen was also helping behind the scenes. I was definitely in the hall with Celyn – waiting to hand out menus and eventually take orders.

We had a set price menu with a choice of four starters and four main courses. The desserts or cheese were chosen from the table and coffee and truffles were also included. I hand-wrote all the menus – these were never to be printed.

Our wine list was small and reasonably priced. We had decided to supply an excellent house wine at a sensible price.

Now we were ready. The woodstove was open, dog sitting in front of it waiting to wag the tail and John ready to open the door for the first car load. This was also to be the 'curtain up' scene for the next ten years!

People duly arrived and admired. The bar was full and I had some orders and took them through to Kate without delay. We had staggered the bookings from half past seven to nine o'clock so that we wouldn't be too panicked. I was almost ready to escort the first table in, when I heard a scream. "A bat, a bat" – that was Georgina. Emily was in the dining room! She must have been nervous too and missed her usual route around, towards the back stairs. Poor Georgie was almost hysterical. I could hear Kate saying "Pull yourself together girl – it's only Emily!" A phrase I was to use quite often!

John had now left the bar and was in the dining room, door closed behind him waving a broom around in the air trying to get Emily into the conservatory. He succeeded, shut the adjoining doors and so managed to get her into the garden. Georgina was screaming, John was shouting and Celyn was barking!

Shirley, in the meantime, was still in the bar playing for time. Scenes from Fawlty Towers came to mind and I was almost good for nothing by now!

Everything calmed down and we all took a deep breath and the evening commenced with no one any the wiser. We had a lot of compliments with no criticisms at all and everyone seemed to enjoy themselves. I know I was glad when it was over. Kate, John, Shirley. Doreen and I had a couple of stiff drinks in the bar, I can tell you. Very pleased with ourselves but exhausted.

At the end of the evening the cloths and napkins went into the laundry and I dried and folded them before falling into bed. At this time we were still in the small bedroom at the top of the back stairs and hadn't yet moved into the big bed-sitting room we were planning.

Now we were really off. We were fully booked for Friday and Saturday and also for our first Sunday lunch. I didn't really want to do Sunday lunch. I thought we would benefit more from a day off but Kate and John wanted to do it so I was outnumbered. We didn't open the restaurant on Sunday nights. Later on, of course, when we had residents, we had to have the restaurant open.

Sunday lunch differed from the evening menu only in the fact that it was traditional 'Sunday dinner'. Still a choice of three starters – one of which was always soup, and a choice of three main courses – one of which was always roast beef and Yorkshire pudding. Then it would be either lamb, pork or chicken with accompanying mint, apple and bread sauce. There was always some sort of fish as a third choice.

I insisted that bread and butter pudding be included in the dessert list. Kate wasn't impressed but produced a wonderful recipe which proved to be so popular that we eventually included it in our evening menu.

Kate's food was magnificent – beautifully tender meat, tasty 'homemade' gravy and fresh vegetables. Plain, but not easy to produce for a large amount of people.

Our Sunday lunches were to bring people from miles around and we became very well known for them throughout Wales and as far away as Bath.

The Friday, Saturday and Sunday went without a hitch. We had waitresses who knew what they were doing, but also friendly and full of personality. Ann and Beryl were to train all the new ones to follow. I always liked the staff to be welcoming and, in later years, the only qualification I insisted on was a smile! I would have an untrained waitress with personality and the customers' well-being as priority rather than a formal fully trained zombie. This policy was never to change and proved a winner.

Consequently, the service was deliberately informal but quietly efficient. I had always hated staff hovering around a table. They intrude on conversations. That is why, from the start, we did not serve the vegetables or the wine but placed both on the table. The wine was always open and ready when people arrived – I hate my wine removed. We were guided totally by our own preferences and enforced them on everyone else!

The first Sunday was my forty-seventh birthday. It passed us by without anyone remembering – not even me!

By the following week we were turning people away which was very upsetting for John. We had to take stock of the number of covers. We could seat a maximum of thirty in the dining room and conservatory but we needed more.

It came to me one night when I was lying awake. We could use the billiard room. It would only mean cancelling the billiard table and shooting down to Pugh's for more tables and chairs. These chairs would have to be covered with blue leather to match the carpet and curtains and we could have dark pink napkins, table-cloths and candles. We would have to look for more brass candlesticks and lace cloths. It was easy. The woodstove was rather in the way, but that didn't matter. I couldn't wait for John to wake up so I could tell him.

He was excited and got totally carried away and waxed lyrical about the small weddings we could do in that room. Oh dear!

The billiard table was cancelled that morning and off we went to Pugh's. Yes, they could get us more tables and chairs fairly quickly.

The tables were proving a great success. They had two pull-out leaves which meant they could seat two people when closed, three with one leaf out and four or six with both leaves out. They also fitted together lengthways for long function or E-shape tables or widthways for a huge oblong table. I had two sizes in both under-cloths and lace so we were extremely versatile. We could seat forty people in an E shape, up to twenty-six on the oblong table and up to thirty-six on individual tables.

I had by this time given up smoking. This wasn't because I was relaxed enough – far from it. I had smoked for years, mainly after meals or when sitting with a coffee and particularly when enjoying a drink. The two things had always gone together. For this reason, I didn't find it particularly difficult – I never had time to sit around anywhere. I was in the bar every evening but taking orders and chatting and it wouldn't have been right with a cigarette.

The next exciting thing to happen was our first resident. William, a friend of ours from Llanrhidian telephoned to see if we were ready. He was Managing Director of I.M.I. in Waunarlwydd and had a colleague visiting who usually stayed in Swansea. Well, we had a few rooms, so, yes we were as ready as we'd ever be.

John Goodyer arrived and we made a great fuss. It turned out that he was quite ill with heart trouble and so was very limited in what he could eat. This didn't throw us at all and Kate did him special meals. He was to visit us at regular intervals over the years and always said he looked forward to Fairyhill and its peace. Sadly, he was to die at a relatively early age.

John was now in overdrive selling Fairyhill. We were in the back of beyond and no one thought we would ever succeed in getting people to find us. He visited all the big industries on the outskirts of Swansea. I also wrote a letter describing what we had to offer and sent hundreds off to companies all over the U.K. We were aiming for businessmen and women as we thought they would need us all year round unlike holiday visitors.

If only we could have one or two from one of the big companies, the word would spread if they liked us, and the rest would follow.

One afternoon, Val came through to the kitchen to say that Petal and Primula had been spotted heading down towards Stembridge. I said, "Come on Kate, follow me," and the next minute saw us running down the lane – Kate in her whites laughing, chasing after the goats. We soon caught them up and, leading one each by the collar up the lane, Kate remarked, "It was never like this in the 'Old School House'."

I was still working hard in the east wing trying to finish off the last five rooms. We now had a dead line for the third week of July. We had taken a booking for our first wedding and they required all of our eleven bedrooms. This was fine as we were only having businessmen as guests and they went home at weekends. I was under a great deal of pressure as after a hard day's work I still had to get changed ready for the restaurant in the evenings.

The billiard room was functioning now which meant we were taking up to sixty-six covers with the two dining rooms and the conservatory. This was to increase again as time went on.

We did employ another decorator to help me with the unfinished bedrooms as it was now obvious I couldn't get them all done and run the business. He did wallpapering and paintwork and that helped a lot. We would just about do it.

Then we had a telephone call which was a real thrill. Frankie Howerd was coming to the Grand Theatre for the second week in July and wanted three rooms with us. He preferred to be in the country rather than a big hotel in town. This was wonderful but it did mean that we had to get our rooms finished a week earlier.

Well, we did it but it meant working many extra hours and going without our sleep. The sign of things to come!

Now we had what we had been waiting for – the arrival of our first 3M businessman. His name was Bob Mandry and he loved everything about Fairyhill. The food, the quiet, the comfort and, as much as anything, he loved our wine list. He was a real foodie and we waited for the flood of fellow colleagues to book in.

On his third visit when we knew him a little better, I broached the subject and explained that we had been looking forward to the outcome of him having spread the word. "Are you serious?" he said. I can see him now sitting in the armchair by the fire with Celyn at his feet. "Do you honestly think I'm telling any of them about this place. It's a closely guarded secret."

What a let down. A big compliment, but not much good for business. He continued with us for years, on many occasions bringing his wife.

Needless to say, we did eventually get more of his colleagues to stay but they found us on their own.

We had lost the billiard room and now we were about to lose our lovely big bed-sitting room.

Luke and John in "Conference Room"

After completion

Someone had asked John if we had a Conference Room. Ooops! This would be a guaranteed way of filling all our bedrooms if there were conference facilities. Not liking to be caught out, he told me that it had come to him in a flash of inspiration. It was perfect – our bedroom!

It would give us a large conference room at the top of the stairs with its own private bathroom and easy access to the kitchen through a second door and down the back stairs. We were expanding by the day.

We found the conference table advertised in the 'Evening Post'. Huge, and in two halves with a lovely black leather top. We bought projector, screen, flip chart and video. All we had to do was to order more blue chairs and we could accommodate twenty in comfort. Back to Pugh's again!

We were now doomed to spend our sleeping time in the tiny back bedroom, one of the two at the top of the back stairs. The second bedroom was intended for my mother, Luke, Joyce, Dobs or any other guests we might have who were prepared to muck in. There was a bathroom between these two rooms and a second bathroom between our room and the conference room. There was also another large room beyond the conference room, directly above the laundry/pot-wash which we had lined with rails and shelves and was referred to as 'the wardrobe'.

It would have been very nice to have had a large bright bedroom where we could have sat in private but as things were to develop we never had any time to sit anywhere. And when it came to sleeping, I don't think we could have cared where we were. Getting horizontal was to be a luxury!

I was finding it more and more difficult to have time for my mother, although I did telephone her every day. I had some after-noons free so would pop in to Mumbles. She liked to go for a drive, so I took her wherever she wanted to go. I often brought her back down to Fairyhill, so she was well up to date with our progress.

She had finally been forced to admit she had been wrong. Not an easy thing for her to do. Now she thought Fairyhill was wonderful and basked a little in all the praise we were getting. More than once, when someone had been congratulating me, she would appear like a proud mother hen saying "This is my daughter – I produced her!"

She often stayed overnight – sometimes through choice but more often because I was too busy to drive her home – a thirty mile round trip. I had pleasure putting her in our best room, if it was available, but more often than not, she was 'up the back stairs' with us. She often came for Sunday lunch when one of the waitresses, usually Beryl, would pick her up then deliver her back home about five o'clock.

She was quite enjoying all the activity and I often regretted that we hadn't done this thirty years earlier. She would have been a real asset to us and would have pitched in anywhere – a real worker.

A situation that kept cropping up with amazing regularity were the people that told how they had 'nearly' bought Fairyhill, or they knew a friend or relation who had 'nearly' bought it. Also, the number who had at that same time told us we must be mad to buy it were now only exceeded by those who said "Gosh, weren't you lucky to get this!"

I feel like giving the same answer to the women who say "Aren't you lucky to be so slim." 'Luck' doesn't come into either situation – it's all down to hard work and determination.

The lower part of the grounds below the trout stream were described on the Ordnance Survey Map as 'water meadow'. From this description you will gather that it was marshy and of no use except to the wildfowl.

John decided it would be wonderful to make a lake. Now, when John has an idea it's no good waiting until the time is opportune – it has to be done immediately.

He went to see Tom at Hill End Farm to ask his advice and whether he could get hold of a machine that could do the job. It would mean getting across the stream and digging out a huge chunk of ground, and building up the banks with what came out of the middle. The whole area would cover about two to three acres and he wanted five small islands left for the ducks to be safe from foxes.

Celyn on first bridge over stream

Yes, it could be done and the work started quickly. I think Tom liked working for us – our jobs were more interesting than the average.

It took a long time and we lost at least one digging bucket. The machine was a huge tracked vehicle and even this got stuck a couple of times and had to be pulled out by a JCB It was eventually finished. It filled naturally by underground springs and what drained out of the hill to the west but took a week or two to complete this.

Everything was not quite right, and John wasn't happy. He was afraid that the bank at the north end was not strong enough and needed to be strengthened. Once again, Tom came and dug away the bank in one area so that the lake emptied into the stream. Now the lake bed and the stream were at one level at this point and Tom went back in with the digger. He was able to make the north bank very much thicker. When he had done this, out he came and built up the bank once more. It was a mammoth job. Now the lake filled once more but because of this short amalgamation of water, the next year we noticed thousands of tiny fish. They were baby brown trout which must have been laid when larger ones found their way in from the stream and became trapped. We hoped they would survive but they apparently like running water rather than a lake and they gradually disappeared. Many to herons, kingfishers and cormorants but mainly because they shouldn't have been there in the first place. Maybe some survived, but we never saw any.

As an after thought we built an inlet channel at the south end leading in from the stream in case of any flooding. It would ease the build up of water at the bend in the river. Then, of course we had to do the same at the top end. We dug two outlet channels and lined them with graduated paving slabs. After a lot of rain the lake could then overflow gradually into the stream. It worked extremely well.

Next, we had to build a bridge to enable us to gain access to the lake. This was made from tree trunks and wooden planks and seemed quite strong. It was at the south end of the lake and was just wide enough to take the tractor and lawn mower. This meant that John could grass and maintain the bank. It eventually developed into a place of unbelievable beauty. A wide grassy walk all around with shady places to sit under the trees. We put a few benches there and it proved very popular with those residents who discovered it.

It didn't take the wild ducks very long to find it and soon there were ducklings paddling around and hiding in the reeds.

Frankie Howerd duly arrived with his manager and accompanist. When he came through the door, I had quite a shock. I thought that the crumpled suit and wig were all part of his stage image but – that's his normal, everyday apparel.

A very quiet man who liked his privacy. He left for the theatre every day late afternoon and came back at about half past ten or eleven. He must have been glad to remove his shoes in the car as he always arrived in his socks. Straight into the bar for triple gin and tonic. He liked Dominic to serve him and they got on very well. He would soon hand back his glass for a double gin to be added. I remember one evening Dobs was in a quandary. He was young and not sure how to handle the situation. The glass had been handed back rather faster than usual. "What's the matter Dobs?" "I haven't got room in the glass for any tonic, Mr. Howerd!"

I wouldn't want to convey that he drank an excessive amount it was just that what most people would spread over an evening, he would drink quickly. I suppose he needed to relax having come straight off stage.

We were lucky in having two dining rooms as sometimes he felt like eating on his own, sometimes just a sandwich in the bar or occasionally joining other people in the dining room.

He enjoyed the quiet of Fairyhill and the consideration we all showed him. He told me that travelling the country staying at big impersonal hotels was very lonely. Sometimes there would be just a friendly waiter to talk to.

He never appeared for breakfast until about eleven o'clock and we had to keep any left over toast for him to take around to the goats. He could be heard approaching the walled garden, calling in that special voice of his "Pet-al, Pet-al". Everything was wonderful until one morning she gave him a push and knocked him over. I don't think he went again, after that!

We enjoyed his visit although it was quite demanding. He thanked us quite profusely on leaving saying what a pleasure it had been to stay at such a friendly place.

Chapter Nine

We now had eleven rooms in action and needed more help. We hadn't up to this stage advertised for staff. Someone always had a friend who wanted to come.

Now we had Marcia from Landimore who played squash with Kate. Her children were in school all day and she was easily persuaded by Kate to take a flexible part-time job. She lived two miles away through the lanes and usually ran to work.

Diane, I had known for years. She, in fact, had worked for John in the Kingsway shop about twenty-five years previously straight from school. She now lived in Rhossili and was married to Roland Button, a farmer. She also had two children, now grown up enough to fend for themselves. Diane would often arrive on her bicycle as indeed would Kate. A very athletic little group.

We also had June who lived around the corner in Burry Alley and helped her husband run a landscape gardening business.

Three very busy ladies, all used to hard work with plenty of common sense.

Marcia would sometimes bring Emma, her fourteen year old daughter who would help with small jobs. We all rubbed along very well together.

Joyce had left. She came to me one lunchtime as she was finishing her shift to say she wouldn't be in again. She was a quiet person and not very forthcoming. It appeared that she didn't like taking orders from anyone other than me. I suppose she had always worked alone and was used to her own system. I was happy with this, but the damage was done. I never knew what really happened, but I lost her. Very sad after all those years together. Nothing I could do would make her stay.

There was a lot more pressure now that we had residents. Claire would come in early to cook breakfasts and John or I would serve them. They were still mostly businessmen who ate breakfast about half past seven – sometimes earlier.

Val would be in the office preparing bills and John, Celyn and I were always in the hall to say thank you to everyone.

I would have already made a list of the bedrooms in use and whether they were to be changed or serviced. Diane and Marcia or whoever was in would have the list and I would inform them as soon as the guest had left. They would then zoom around for all sheets, pillowcases and towels and I would get the laundry into action.

As we got more into the swing of things, the girls would make their own cleaning rota and depending on how many rooms were booked, they would put their names down and decide which days they wanted to work. This meant that they could swap around to suit themselves and if we suddenly got busier, they would ring each other for help. It worked brilliantly from everyone's point of view and we never felt the need to alter this system.

Also, I think because we were all women, we were more versatile. My experience is that most men can only do one thing at a time whereas women who have run a family are constantly thinking ahead as well as doing several things at once!

As time progressed, it meant that a lot of the girls, as well as cleaning, would waitress, potwash or go into the kitchen. There was always a great atmosphere – we got on well and there was a lot of laughing.

I was now more relaxed about my home being full of strangers. I was, however, concerned about Celyn being in the bar and constantly called her to come out.

One evening I was standing in front of the woodstove in the hall chatting away to a guest. I must have been calling Celyn and he eventually asked me why I didn't leave her alone. I remarked that I was afraid there might be someone who didn't like dogs. He immediately said "My deah, you don't want that type here!"

It made me think and I really had to agree. He was absolutely right. From then on she behaved in the proper way – as though she were at home. I can only remember one person ever objecting to her, and we didn't like him either!

In fact, she proved to be our biggest asset. She relaxed anxious businessmen waiting for important colleagues and sat at the side of all single guests to make them feel welcome.

As soon as the first guest arrived in the bar of an evening, she would bark for a beer mat. John would flick this into the air and she would catch it, then take it to everyone in turn for them to throw it out of the bar and across the hall.

Some evenings the men would have competitions to see who could flick the beer mat from the hall, down the corridor and into the dining room – a distance of about twenty-five yards – with Celyn tearing up and down 'fetching'.

In the mornings she would wait on the first floor landing and accompany each guest down to breakfast and sit under their tables in turns. Everyone loved Celyn.

Towards the end of this first summer we were approached by the local artist, Gareth Thomas, asking if we could host an exhibition on a Friday evening. John was all for this but I didn't want to do it as we were very busy in the restaurant that night with both dining rooms full and for me, that was enough to cope with.

Gareth then went on to say that it would only be about twenty-five people at six o'clock, so I relented.

It was held upstairs in the Conference room. We removed the big table so there was plenty of room to lay out nibbles and drinks and for people to mill around.

What a disaster! About a hundred people must have arrived. He assured me he had never had that many previously. They all wanted a free chance to give Fairyhill the once over.

We got into a terrible mess because when our diners started arriving at half past seven there wasn't room to park and quite a lot just drove off.

I couldn't differentiate between people who had booked in for a meal and Gareth's guests who seemed to be everywhere, except in the Conference room! I had to wait until someone asked for a menu.

We were always so desperate to please everyone, I couldn't bear it when something went wrong, like this. It was a hard lesson to learn but I made sure it never happened again.

Kate was, at thirty-one, very active and would often cycle into work from Mumbles. She was very highly strung and extremely competitive so everything was done at full speed. She got through a tremendous volume of work and before leaving would have organised the following day. All shopping lists and rotas were done and whoever was in first knew what they had to get on with.

The atmosphere in the kitchen was mostly light hearted with a great deal of laughter but of course, there was the occasional panic. She was an extremely happy and bubbly person most of the time.

She was a dedicated foodie and often spent her days off driving a couple of hundred miles to a restaurant she'd heard of. She had a girl friend in London so would shoot off there after work on many a Saturday night in search of new ideas. She had her finger well and truly on the pulse.

She spent one week working with Albert Roux in Le Gavroche where she gained a lot of knowledge from that lovely man, and also another week with Marco Pierre White who she thought brilliant but not such a lovely man. She came back on both occasions with lots of ideas and a list of new equipment she wanted!

We were beginning to get quite a lot of company business now and they would have large dinner parties with us.

Our dining rooms were proving to be very versatile. We could use the Billiard room for large dinner parties seating up to twenty-four around an oblong table with private bar and entertainment. Many nights we had a group of our Pontardulais choir 'boys' to sing and entertain visitors. These evenings were a hit with all nationalities from East or West and did much to cement many business deals, I'm sure.

If we had a private party in the Billiard room it still left us the dining room and conservatory for residents and outside diners. We also often covered the conference table with our cloths and used that as a private dining room. This proved invaluable for family parties up to twenty as any children were free to run around without fear of disturbing others. The private bathroom there was also a big success. I didn't really mind now that this wasn't my bedroom!

Having two dining rooms also meant that with careful planning, one could accommodate early diners and one late. Consequently, as soon as the early room was vacant we would change the table-cloths and lay up for breakfast. Apart from laying the tables, the waitresses would prepare butter – one pot for each table – put out the fruit and cereals and lastly, squeeze the oranges. The oranges took a great deal of time and were tedious but we did it for many years until 'Freshly Squeezed Orange Juice' finally appeared in Sainsbury's. This was a great break through!

I can honestly boast that no one dining late at Fairyhill ever witnessed the laying-up of breakfast. It's a practice done by restaurants that has always irritated me. As though they are telling me it's time to leave.

Usually, the waitresses were never later than half past eleven. John and I did anything that cropped up after that. Serving drinks, clearing tables and carrying out to the potwash.

John would be hovering around the bar area in case he was needed which left me free to get on with the laundry, between serving liqueurs or making more coffee when required. All napkins and cloths from the early dining room were done before I went to bed and all kitchen cloths, chefs' whites and tea towels were put on overnight and dried in the morning. The poor pot wash was always last to leave and sometimes locked up.

Our waitresses had now increased from Beryl and Ann to include Sheila with Marcia and Claire helping when necessary. Sheila again lived locally in Llanmadoc and was very versatile and, like the rest of us, pitched in with whatever was needed.

Sheila had three sons, and the eldest, Ian was roped in to potwash. This, I have always thought to be one of the hardest jobs in catering and must not be demeaned. It really sorts the wheat from the chaff and one has to apply stamina, determination, method and speed. I reckon a good potwasher will go far in life. I have done it on many occasions and know what I'm talking about. Some people just can't make it. I insisted very early on that the potwash had a share of the tips, which doesn't normally happen in restaurants.

We were still accommodating mostly businessmen which was relatively easy. They would arrive about half past six and be back down in the bar for a drink before eating. Most would enjoy a chat and indeed, some nights were hilarious. It was rare to have late nights during the week as they were usually up for early breakfasts and would be ready to leave by eight o'clock. This meant the girls could make an early start to get home at a reasonable time. It also kept the wages bill down.

Everyone had a weekly time card which they filled in themselves and added up the hours before handing in to Val.

At the start we had divided the tips out every evening and handed them out there and then. We were soon hauled over the coals by the Tax Office and made to feel like criminals defrauding the country. From then on the tips had to be paid with the wages with the appropriate tax taken out. Nothing is simple!

One of our biggest fans proved to be a gentleman who was starting up a business in Swansea and consequently stayed with us one or two nights every week or so. He absolutely loved everything about Fairyhill – the food, the house, the grounds, Celyn, the staff and us.

Pat Roach was very outgoing and confident and really made himself at home. We looked forward to seeing him.

Because we had done so much work on the house he wanted to know every detail and had peeked into every nook and cranny inside and out from cellar, scullery and kitchen to attic, stable and goathouse! He had slept in every bedroom and enjoyed eating his breakfast in the kitchen.

We often came across Pat showing people around the house, explaining exactly how we had done various things. He was so proud of us and loved the house.

He brought many people to stay with us over the years and he always said that one day he would own something like Fairyhill and we had changed the course of his life.

It transpired that he eventually did decide to buy a hotel. It was, he said, quite ordinary, but when he got it going, he would sell it, buy a better one and continue in that way until he got what he wanted – something like Fairyhill!

The thing that amused me was his comment that he would have to go into it seriously, "Because Midge, you and John only run it as a hobby – it's so laid back."

I said, "Patrick, if we give you and everyone else that impression, then we are doing a damned good job!" If he could only see how I run around once out of sight! Chatting to people is vital but extremely time consuming and the time always has to be made up.

We were still in contact with him after his first three hotels but then lost touch. I would think he's either bankrupt or a millionaire!

By this time Frank had left us and moved on but Martin, Roddy and Mark were well on with the Coach House. We hadn't altered it much. We had to remove the huge double coach doors and stone up the hole, first putting in two new windows to match the five existing ones. The big doors were cut down to make new ones for the Bothey House.

We had to search the junk yards for some more old internal doors, banisters, spindles and newel posts.

We built on a large porch, put in a kitchen, bathroom and three small bedrooms. We could either let it for self catering or as a family unit on a bed and breakfast basis. It only had one bathroom so we had to be quite selective as to who shared. It proved to be very versatile.

Coach House in original state

After "facelift"

Now that we had such a busy restaurant, we had to be selective on the weddings we took. Most people like to stay on for the evening but this would have meant closing the restaurant and upsetting regulars which we didn't want to do. We had struggled hard to get people to travel to us and we didn't want to risk losing them.

We overcame this by only accepting small eleven o'clock weddings – a maximum of forty guests who were happy to leave at half past five. This gave us time to clean up and be ready for the evening.

We could keep these small weddings very intimate, letting them enjoy the run of Fairyhill, having it totally to themselves. We weren't doing lunches at this stage – only the occasional private party – so there would be no one else around.

The drawing room was spacious enough for guests to mingle and chat whilst the photographers were busy in the grounds. Hopefully, the weather would be fine so the french doors were open for people to spill out onto the lawn.

I always kept myself aware of what an important day it was for the family and tried to make everything special. They would be ready to eat by two o'clock or earlier if requested, and I don't think they ever felt rushed.

My mad rush was on as soon as they had left because inevitably, it would be a Saturday and we would be fully booked for the evening.

I had to get all the cloths and napkins into the laundry, dried and folded ready to go back on an hour later. In the meantime, one of the girls (or me if there was no one available) would be vacuuming through and cleaning all the toilets. Please don't let there be any confetti!

I would have already planned and arranged the tables and got the cloths back on by half past six when the evening waitresses came in.

If I was lucky I would have half an hour to shower and change to be back down and ready for the first guests.

Sometimes I would be so tired, I thought I would never make it through the night. My legs wouldn't carry me! Beryl had given me a good waitresses' tip – "Keep changing your shoes." It did help, but I needed more shoes!

I would go to the bar exhausted to meet John in the same state. The amazing thing was that once we heard the first car arrive, we would be alert and smiling as though someone had said 'Curtain up'. The next thing we knew it was eleven o'clock and people were starting to leave.

Not the end for me though, The laundry from the 'early' dining room would have already been almost done and the girls would be laying for breakfast. As soon as the second room was empty I would go through the same routine as the afternoon but now preparing the tables ready for Sunday lunch.

At this time I could now go to bed but as time progressed I was to be cooking Sunday lunch so would have to get all the laundry washed, dried and folded before going to bed – sometimes three o'clock.

Kate had also been working long hours and had been taking days off randomly without being able to plan too far in advance.

She had been training Alison, Claire and Rhian and we decided that they should take over Sunday lunch – Alison on main courses. We had also taken on Jennifer. She was to come in full time. She could have Sundays off but would do Monday night instead of Kate. This meant that Kate had every Sunday and Monday off.

Needless to say, I was very anxious about the lunch but Alison was full of confidence and indeed everything went without a hitch as did Monday nights with Jennifer.

Kate's food had been a success from the start and we were having compliments from all quarters.

One thing we were not totally happy about was the beef. At the beginning we were buying whole sirloins and cutting them into steaks. We then served them with various sauces. The sirloins were bought from a firm in Bristol and they proved to be much too unpredictable. John and I were always afraid to ask people if they were tender! We tried local butchers and eventually decided to change from sirloin to fillet. This was far more expensive but a wise decision.

Shirley, Kate's father, was still helping John out in the bar, when we were busy, Dobs having now left us to go to Australia. Shirley was great and had a charming, chatty manner. Doreen, Kate's mother would often be somewhere in the kitchen area. She was more retiring and happy to keep well out of the public eye. I was only sorry that my mother couldn't be part of it all.

We were already far busier than we ever dreamt – what had happened to my leisurely bed and breakfast?

We needed to be busy – we had borrowed what seemed to me a vast sum of money. We couldn't refuse anything – weddings, conferences, christenings, presentations, clay pigeon shoots. We even held a cricket match which was played down on the parkland. This was between two local pubs and we laid out a buffet and drinks in the conservatory. It was a scorching afternoon and proved to be a perfect setting.

I don't know how long it would take us to break even. We seemed to have so many staff, but again, our system meant that they were only 'in' when needed. I would have to continue to do as much as I could myself.

The thought often crossed my mind that running a pub would have been so much easier!

Chapter Ten

After six months we had exciting news – we were in 'The Good Food Guide'. This would help put us on the map. No one could find us. No one had heard of us. We had no passing trade so people would have to search. What a handicap. Never mind, we were getting there. Be welcoming and friendly to everyone and they would tell their friends how lovely we were!

In addition to 'The Good Food Guide', we were also a member of 'Welsh Rarebits'. This was a publication produced by a small group of hoteliers like us who owned their own business. It was organised by Emyr Griffiths who used to be with the Welsh Tourist Board but now this was his brain-child. At the time of joining, it had just started with only about fifteen hotels but it proved to be a great success and brought us mainly Americans. Since that time Welsh Rarebits has expanded but the standards are high and only the best privately run hotels are accepted.

Derek Johannsen also paid us a visit and we agreed to go into his publication 'Recommended Hotels'.

He said he wasn't only concerned with the standard and appearance of an hotel but was more interested in the welcome and general ambience and the way that guests were treated.

He was a very nice gentleman and visited us regularly until he became quite ill and eventually sold his magazine. He subsequently recovered and a few years later started a new publication called 'Connoisseurs' Choice'.

We had now changed our wine merchant. We had been with Luc Lucerre in Cardiff but now, a friend of ours, Brian Johnson, had started his own wine business and we felt we would like to support him. It was mutually beneficial and he looked after us well. We told him we wanted a small list. I think the average person is confused by a long wine list and anyway, it takes up too much time to read through!

He agreed, and guided us expertly until we arrived at exactly the right balance. Our house wines were sensibly priced on the low side and we had a good mix with a variety of prices. We worked on the principle that if the wine was not overpriced, then people might have a second bottle.

Over the years, we were complimented time and again on our wine list and their fair prices and we were always grateful to Brian for looking after us so well. Soon after starting up his company, 'Celtic Vintner', he was voted Welsh Wine Merchant of the Year, an award that he was to win for many years to come.

By the time autumn approached in this first year we were settling more into the routine. I was exhausted every night but things were becoming slightly less tense. I was still extremely anxious about the table planning and always tried to anticipate any unforeseen situation that could arise, such as an extra person turning up unexpectedly on an already crowded table. As it happened, I was never to recover from this anxiety. It was probably what kept me permanently on my toes.

Three mornings a week John would go on his shopping round. First stop Nancy Morgan in Swansea for the bread. Lovely old-fashioned bread baked every day – not steamed. Next, he picked up the cream from a dairy in the dock area. He would telephone in advance for this to be left inside the locked dairy as the staff finished early morning. He had been given a key so that was easy. The fish market was his next call then, armed with a long list it was off to the Cash and Carry. He knew all the recurring basics but a list was permanently pinned to the notice board in the kitchen and everyone added bits and pieces to it. He was good at this and was usually back by lunchtime.

Apart from the shopping round he was spending most of the time in the grounds building up our stock of wood for the stoves. He had seeded the orchard since it had been cleared so there was a lot of extra grass to cut. The sheep were keeping a lot of it down but there was a limit how much they could eat!

John would come in from outside to be washed and changed by half past five, ready for anyone who might arrive. Val would have left at half past three so we relied on Celyn between times to bark if anyone arrived! She really was good at it. People would often ask if she was a working collie and we always said, "Certainly, she's our P.R. Officer."

When Val had left for home the telephone would be answered either in the bar, office or kitchen. Having three answering points meant that it was always answered quickly even if two lines were engaged. The reservations book would be kept out in the kitchen during the evening and everyone was familiar with the procedure of taking a booking.

Once John was 'on duty' I would pop upstairs for an hour (hopefully) and prepare for the evening. Before going for my break, I would have made out a list of bookings on my order pad – name and number of persons – and then stand little name cards on the tables. I made sure I had a note of any spare tables as sometimes people would ring late or even arrive without booking. For this reason, we always prepared an extra ten portions of vegetables. The meat and fish were all cooked to order but it takes time to prepare vegetables.

The waitresses arrived at half past six. I had already arranged the tables with cloths and flowers so all they had to do was lay up and prepare the butter, desserts and cheeseboard. Incidentally, Martin's cheeseboard was a great success.

As our bedroom was just at the top of the back stairs above the kitchen, I could hear exactly what was happening so if there were any queries, I was down like a shot.

There was always a lot of laughter and good humour at this time of the evening – the waitresses chatting away to the kitchen staff. As the evening progressed, there was less time for chat.

I had learnt not to take bookings after half past nine. My experience was that people who ate later than that had usually been drinking a lot beforehand. They were 'night people' and didn't leave until about two o'clock. It couldn't be helped if residents stayed up late chatting – we could tell them to help themselves and put lights out when they went to bed.

Because we didn't take late bookings this meant that the kitchen staff had finished by ten o'clock. The waitresses served the cheese and desserts, so once the last main course had gone out and they had cleaned down the chefs were free to go. They had exceptional hours for a busy hotel kitchen – half past two until ten with no split shifts.

Kate sometimes stayed on to prepare something or other and if we had a lunch the next day she preferred to prep up as much as possible rather than come in early in the morning.

By this time I was cooking all breakfasts. Claire had been doing this but she had now left and it would have meant Kate doing a split shift.

I was very nervous at first and was up out of bed far too early. Kate had always pre-cooked bacon, sausages and tomatoes and put them in the hot cupboard ready for the orders. I soon found this was far too wasteful of food and electricity and started cooking everything to order.

John was serving breakfasts and we were a good little team. We would have already asked everyone the night before whether they needed an early morning call so we knew the time of the earliest breakfast. We set our own call accordingly.

Celyn would meet them on the first floor landing and escort them down when John took their order. I would already have all my plates warmed, tomatoes and mushrooms portioned in dishes and my bacon ready for grilling. The sausages had been removed from the menu as they took too long to cook.

John gave me the order and then took out tea or coffee and placed bread in the toaster. Nancy Morgan bread made the best toast! If I had fried bread on my order I would ask him to cut me a slice.

We soon got into the rhythm and it wasn't too bad. At this time we were still catering mainly for single people which meant a maximum of eleven breakfasts. Little did I know I would end up doing as many as forty!

Val was in the office by half past seven so John didn't have to worry about giving out bills. He would have these made up the night before all ready for Val.

We always had a very personal relationship with our residents and many of them became friends. We treated guests as though they were in our home, which of course, they were, and made a conscious effort not to be remote or formal. Either John or I was always on hand and both of us, plus Celyn were in the hall to say thank you and goodbye. We thought that however successful an evening had been, the last impressions are what stay in the memory.

One very regular guest who was besotted with Celyn and always took her for a walk when he arrived, told us one morning that he had been wakened during the night by Celyn 'knocking' on his door. He had, of course, let her in. I apologised but actually, he was delighted and made the remark that "After all, it's not like a real hotel." I know he meant it as a compliment and it was exactly the feel we were hoping to achieve.

We had our first American visitors about six months after opening. Like many others, they had come across us by accident and couldn't believe how narrow our approach lane was. They were even more shocked when they learnt that it wasn't one-way. "What happens if we meet a car coming towards us?" We told them, as we told most timid visitors, not to worry as most locals could reverse as fast as they could go forward and would be glad to do so as long as they were thanked with a smile!

When John was serving these Americans at breakfast, he came into the kitchen laughing. "It's like Tom and Jerry out there!" he said.

Apparently, they were admiring the view out through the window when Martha Gatwick went running past – half flying with a fox in close pursuit. Everyone left the breakfast room and rushed to the front door in time to see them both hurtling past. I, by this time had shot out through the kitchen door to meet them in the courtyard when the fox gave up and ran off towards the farmyard across the road.

Martha Gatwick was glad to get into the kitchen, through the scullery and out into the big walled garden where she was supposed to be locked in with the others.

I don't know whether it was this shock and exertion that was too much for her or whether it would have been old age but I found her dead in the garden a few days later. We had a good cry and a funeral. She deserved a good send off. She was a chicken in a million!

At this point we decided to give the rest of our chickens to a farmer friend in Landimore. Although we had about two dozen, because they were free range, they hardly laid any eggs in the winter and even on full lay there hadn't been nearly enough to supply the needs of the kitchen. Apart from this, in the back of our minds, we always had the fear of rats.

We had been lucky with our staff – most of them living locally and all getting on well together.

Alison, who was cooking Sunday lunch with Rhian had now been offered a full-time job in Swansea University kitchens so, of course, she couldn't refuse that.

Her sister Lis, waitressed for us occasionally and we managed to persuade her to take over the lunches. She had worked with her mother, Marjorie Beynon when managing the 'King's Head' in Llangennith so was well used to a kitchen.

Lis had two children but they were looked after by Andrew, her husband.

There had been a stray black kitten hanging about the courtyard for days and in spite of my threats, someone had been feeding it. The poor thing was tiny and it was soon curled up in the staff room.

I took it to the vet to have it checked over and it wasn't a kitten but fully grown. It was so small, I called him 'Dwt' which I have always translated as 'Dot'. He soon made himself at home much to Winni's disgust and was often to be found in the drawing room on someone's lap. I thought he had settled in well but after a few months he must have decided to move on and left us.

One afternoon, I received a very agitated call from my sister to say my mother had fallen and broken her wrist. She was still in the hospital with a friend where she had been taken by ambulance.

She had fallen a few months previously and Jo had moved into her flat for five weeks to take care of her. Now Jo's son was ill and her time was accounted for. Anyway, she had done her stint, now it was my turn.

I leapt into my car and was gone. My only thought was to bring her to Fairyhill. She was so shocked, and shaking from head to toe.

I brought her straight home and put her to bed in room 212. Lots of tea and a sleep. Everyone made a fuss of her and she soon felt better.

Anyone who has broken a wrist knows how difficult it is to wash, dress or – for a woman, go to the loo, so she had to be helped with everything.

I went back to her flat next morning with a list of things to collect and she stayed until the plaster came off.

She was more than comfortable – breakfast in bed every morning and the girls taking it in turns to pop in for a chat. June loved talking to my mother and could often be found in her room, taking a long time to clean it.

Of course, she was up for most of the day but retired early evening before we got busy. She had her own television and could make a cup of tea or coffee whenever she pleased. She could ring down when she wanted something and was always taken a large gin and tonic before her dinner. She'd never had it so good!

She really enjoyed herself and I was glad to do it. Nevertheless, I think she was quite relieved to get back to her own home when she was better, although she did miss the company.

It was about November, eight months after opening that we appeared in the 'Guide Michelin'. We were, of course, thrilled as they had awarded us a red rocking chair which meant a secluded hotel in peaceful surroundings. This was to bring us more French visitors than anything else but also some Dutch and Italian.

All we wanted now was a visit from Egon Ronay.

We were to come more adept later at spotting inspectors but at this time, with most of our guests single gentlemen, it was virtually impossible.

Christmas was looming and we were taking bookings for parties. Friday nights were proving to be what everyone wanted, so these were soon filled.

The maximum we could take in one big party was forty and we would ask them to arrive at half past eight. By that time, we would have all our other diners booked in with most of them already eating. This would leave the drawing room empty and free for the large party to have their pre-dinner drinks and chat. They would then move to the Billiard room by nine o'clock leaving the drawing room available once more for any of the earlier diners who might want their coffee there.

It took a lot of stage managing but it always seemed to work and no one was kept waiting.

On a few occasions we had two large parties so I would have to persuade one to eat early. I always found if I was honest and explained things, people were quite happy.

Having these parties from the end of November meant that I had to decorate early. I refused to start before December but then I had to get cracking. What a mammoth job. Why couldn't I be happy with the usual tinsel and Father Christmas's like most other public places?

I have always used fresh greenery but here, I needed so much. I collected hundreds of fir cones, sprayed them gold then tied them in groups. These I hung everywhere – hall, bar, drawing room, dining room, stairs, passageways and billiard room. I also had to do the conference room as we had parties there too. I had masses of greenery everywhere – yew, holly and fir. Because this was all done so early, it kept dying and had to be replaced two or three times before Christmas.

The billiard room has a high sloping ceiling up to a central sky light. It's very high and my mind flashed back to when I teetered on Frank's scaffolding. I almost came to grief again, climbing up to pin decorations on the beams and all around the high ceiling windows. I did cheat here and used a mass of artificial holly and fir but it was so high and the effect was fine. I couldn't possibly keep climbing up there every week to replace dead branches – once was enough! I dreaded this chore every year. People were very complimentary so that made it all worthwhile.

Our first Christmas was a smash hit! We had been totally booked from the end of October but I nevertheless took a waiting list of two's, threes, fours and sixes so we were covered for any cancellations. I did this whenever we were fully booked.

I think that first Christmas we were about sixty and most of these were regulars.

Everyone arrived at half past twelve and went into the drawing room for complimentary champagne and general chat to get everyone friendly. I had done a room plan for both dining rooms so everyone knew where they were sitting.

It was a set seven course meal so as soon as I had taken wine orders and it was on the tables, I herded them in to eat.

We had splashed out on crackers and everyone seemed to have amazing presents. There was a wonderful atmosphere. John and I joined in with the waitresses but still had time to spend with every table.

No one seemed to want to go home and it was six o'clock by the time the last had left. We had sent the waitresses home a lot earlier as they wanted to get back to their families and anyway, they were on triple time!

We had planned to have our meal at six. Kate's parents had come to join us and we all sat down eventually in the dining room about seven o'clock. We were all tired but poor Kate was exhausted and drained and couldn't wait to get home. She had excelled herself.

Boxing Day was our only day off in the year!

Chapter Eleven

January and February 1986 proved to be busier than we thought. During the week the restaurant went quiet but Saturday nights were busy and we were always full for lunch on Sundays.

We could spare the time to take Celyn for the odd walk, catch up with some decorating and small repairs and generally take stock. I could also spend a little time with my mother who would often stay the odd night with us.

Kate had been saying that she needed more fridge space; then she could prepare more in advance. She would also like a bigger freezer as this would make life easier. There always seemed to be something more she needed; copper pans and pots, ice-cream machine, iron pans, wicker steamers. As long as they paid for themselves it didn't matter.

The fridge and freezer were ordered and duly arrived. They were enormous and took up a great chunk of wall. They had to come down into the bottom half of the kitchen which I thought of as mine.

This half held a big wooden table and chairs from the kitchen in Burry Cottage. John and I had our breakfast here (if we were lucky) and a couple of hours later all the cleaning girls had their coffee break. We all sat around the table chatting for fifteen or twenty minutes eating any left over toast there might be. I never had to tell them to get started. Someone would always get up and say "Come on, let's get cracking." John often joined us – he couldn't bear missing out on anything.

To the side of the kitchen table, on the wall, was a rack for the red wine. This was large enough to hold three bottles of every bin thus ensuring that I always had enough at the right temperature. There was also a refrigerator for the white wine, again storing three of each bin, Every night I would replace what had been sold from the cellar.

At the far end of the kitchen was a huge Welsh dresser. It had been made by John's grandfather and touched the ceiling. People had to walk past the kitchen to reach the billiard room, so could look straight down to the spotlighted dresser. I always thought it looked so lovely and gave a more relaxed and homely look to the kitchen. The functional, cooking part was hidden from their view.

Since the chickens had left, Petal and Primula had the big walled garden to themselves. They refused to eat any of the weeds which were in abundance, so John had to go in with the lawn-mower.

Brookie had told me where to buy the hay they liked – only the best, organic!

Even taking all this into account, Primula was not well. I knew there was something wrong when she didn't rush out of the goat house one morning. She lay around all day looking miserable. I telephoned Brookie and she gave me the number of her vet. He didn't seem to know what was wrong but gave her an injection and also left some with me so that I could give her a dose the next two

Our lake from northern end

days. He showed me what to do and I managed it the following day. I hated doing it and it took me a while to pluck up courage. John buries his head in his hands if he sees a needle so was of no help at all. He kept well out of the way!

The third day was a Sunday and as usual, we had a crowd booked for lunch. There was always so much to do beforehand and I still hadn't given Primula her jab. As luck would have it, some friends of ours, Bob and Ann, were entertaining a guest whom I knew to be a dentist. Having given them all complimentary drinks he found it difficult to refuse when I asked him if he would help me with Primula's injection or, more to the point – give it to her!

We all trooped out into the walled garden after lunch and the deed was duly done.

Unfortunately, poor Primula never did recover and gradually deteriorated. I called the vet again but there was nothing he could do. Another funeral.

We gave Petal to someone locally who had many goats. I didn't have the heart to keep her on her own. She is still leading a happy and healthy life.

We had a brilliant idea for the now redundant goat house. It was dismantled and carried to the far side of the lake. We erected it and put in a couple of chairs and it was ideal for a hide. We never had much time to use it but quite a lot of our guests did and reported to us all that they saw. It was also such a lovely place just to sit quietly.

Our staff was still increasing. In the kitchen were two more of Kate's friends. Jane and Jenny from Rhossili who were also glad of flexible hours to fit in with their children. Diane, who was still clean-ing was now, more and more in the kitchen, so between them all there were enough to have a workable rota which suited everyone.

Lis was still cooking Sunday lunch either with Rhian, Diane, Jenny or Jane. If they needed a third in the kitchen, Annette would always be ready to help. Annette was a farmer's wife also and lived in Llangennith.

Although no one was qualified at all, they were all sensible women who enjoyed cooking and knew all the basics. Kate soon had them trained in the ways of restaurant cooking, which has many different techniques. They loved all this extra knowledge and considered themselves quite privileged to have the opportunity. Most of them hadn't had a job since having their children and they were glad of the confidence they were gaining, as well as enjoying the company and the money.

We were still alright on the cleaning side with Marcia, Diane, Sheila and June. Sometimes Marcia and June would bring daughters Emma and Dawn for reinforcements. Emma and Marcia were always prepared to waitress. In fact, everyone was extremely flexible. We were so lucky.

The next to knock on our door was Terry, or more to the point, Terry's wife Ann. She asked if we had a vacancy for 'a clever man who could do most things.' I passed this offer over to John, and Terry duly arrived for a trial. We never believed in references. The only way to see if things work out is to watch people in action. Qualifications don't impress me very much – common sense is worth far more. None of our staff had qualifications but I wouldn't have changed any of them.

More substantial new bridge

Terry was to stay with us for a number of years and apart from working in the grounds, was able to cope with all minor repairs that seem to crop up regularly. He was also able to fathom the extremely complicated plumbing system at Fairyhill.

The first year he was with us we had a very bad storm and that, combined with a high tide, resulted in our river flooding badly. It was so high and turbulent that it washed away our main bridge and a smaller ornamental one onto the island. Terry rebuilt the smaller one as a stone arch which looked lovely. The bigger one was more substantial and needed to be very strong.

John found the wood for this in Swansea where a demolition firm were removing an old warehouse in the docks area. There were wonderful pitch pine timbers in the roofs and he bought them all. They even agreed to deliver. As luck would have it, they measured thirty feet which was the exact length we needed to span the river.

Terry not only replaced the bridge that was washed away but he and John also constructed a second one lower down and both these were strong enough to carrying anything.

In addition to all his other jobs, Terry was stocking up the wood pile which meant John could take things easier.

Our rooms, during the week, seemed constantly full with businessmen. We had a lot from 3M in Gorseinon, Morganite in Morriston (our two favourites) and various other firms in and around Swansea.

They were mostly regulars and enjoyed staying with us. I would do all their laundry, free of charge, and they would tell each other about Fairyhill and arrange to meet up. We had some great evenings with lots of laughter and leg-pulling.

Sometimes we couldn't cope with them all. In addition to our eleven rooms, we now had three in the Coach House, which they were happy to share if they knew each other – even though there was only one bathroom.

If all these rooms were full and we had a request from someone we knew well, we would let them have our spare room at the top of the back stairs and many times we even moved out of our own bedroom! This meant we had to sleep on a sofa bed in the staff room and wash in the scullery! We needed all the money we could get and it was hard to turn people away when we had fought so hard to get them.

Kate had been ski-ing for a couple of weeks – a well earned holiday. Kim, from Catering College, had come in every evening to cover for her. I think he found it quite different working in a busy kitchen after years of teaching but no doubt, it was good experience. Everything went smoothly and on her return Kate suggested we took a few days off. She would look after everything.

We were extremely tired and decided to book into a Health Farm in Somerset for a complete rest. It was very expensive and really, a total waste of time. We slept through most of it! In retrospect, we should have rested for a couple of days and then booked in there for a complete overhaul. We could have enjoyed the sauna, swimming pool, massage and general pampering to rejuvenate ourselves. Indeed, I think my feet needed a retread!

Kate had been looking after things at Fairyhill and we had left copious lists of routine things to see to. We were so meticulous. One thing she forgot to do was to book in everyone's morning call. The man in room 212 was furious and turned out to be an Egon Ronay inspector. He made a point of informing Kate of this fact as if to get his own back! That was the end of our hopes for an entry. We had to wait another two years to live that down but then we were accepted.

It really put us off even thinking about going away. We would worry more than it was worth.

We had a five day booking from a television film crew that summer. They were to film part of an advertisement for the Electricity Board and they asked if we had a helicopter pad. We very firmly said "Yes", and were able to give them a grid reference.

They told us that they would be bringing two helicopters, a large one to be in the commercial and a smaller one to film it. I absolutely adore helicopters and was so excited – I could hardly wait!

We were to expect them 'some time in the morning'. I found it difficult to get on with anything and kept rushing outside, thinking I could hear an engine. Eventually, one appeared quite quickly from the West over the trees and swept past. I was mortified! Hadn't they spotted my white sheet weighed down in each corner with a stone? It was in the middle of the parkland – they couldn't possibly miss it! I ran down across the lawn and over the ha-ha and, sure enough, it was returning, and now couldn't possibly miss me, jumping up and down on the sheet, waving my arms!

What a pilot – he hovered over the landing place then proceeded to fly, inches from the ground, over the ha-ha and the lawn to park on the path right outside the drawing room! The second helicopter arrived about an hour later and I went through the whole procedure again! Our lawn was swept very clear of leaves.

Shortly afterwards, the rest of the party arrived, together with a petrol tanker holding an ample supply of fuel.

Over the years we were to have many more private helicopters and although I was always thrilled none of them quite lived up to this initial excitement.

This was the first of many film crews and we thoroughly enjoyed them. They told us that most hotels hated having them as they disrupted the place so much. In our case it didn't matter. They had taken all our rooms so there were no other guests to disturb. The Conference Room was chock-a-block with film equipment of all sorts.

I got a big kick from seeing the helicopters parked outside and showed them off to every diner that arrived. Needless to say, I watched every take off and landing.

Suffice it to say that the highlight of this visit was my trip in a helicopter. I was promised this as soon as they arrived but the days were passing and nothing was forthcoming. On the last day I just had to bring up the subject – I was desperate. The pilot was very apologetic and said he would take me straight away – with two others. I rushed into the kitchen to tell the girls. Kate and Jane were there – "Oh, can we come, can we come ? Pleeese … Midgie." John had intended having a trip but he very gallantly gave in. The three of us rushed out as the rotors were whirring and climbed in – both girls in their chefs' whites, complete with hats. "WAIT," said Kate, and rushed back to the kitchen to take the meringues out of the oven!

We were really excited, swooping quickly down across the lawn then up and over the trees. Fairyhill looked lovely. He took us all around Gower, passing low over Jane's house in Rhossili. We weren't away very long – about twenty minutes probably which was just as well as it was now half past five – a busy time in the kitchen.

Jane telephoned her son as soon as she returned and asked him why he hadn't brought in the laundry from the line. He couldn't believe that his Mum had been in the helicopter!

After all the cost of a whole crew staying for five days with expensive food and wine, when the advertisement was eventually shown, our bit took about two seconds and really, the Electricity helicopter could have been flying over any coastline, not necessarily Gower!

One interesting thing that happened on that visit was that one of the photographers was an entomologist and asked if he could set up a moth trap overnight in the woods. This meant a large cloth 'dish' with a light to attract the moths. He told us the next morning that he had counted forty different species and was amazed. Fairyhill had been neglected and undisturbed for so many years that it was a real haven for all animals and wildlife.

We were getting quite a few conferences now. Some just for the day, arriving at nine o'clock until about half past five but others over two or three days. These were a lot more demanding. It meant coffee when they arrived and again at half past ten, lunch at half past twelve then tea and biscuits at four o'clock. The dinner in the evening was no problem.

Because the Conference Room was directly above the kitchen, I had discovered that the sound travelled up through the ceiling – which was open beamed. I wouldn't let the girls talk loudly, have the radio on or use any mixers. They had to go out into the pot wash. It was a great strain on everyone but we had to be considerate.

On fine, sunny days, I would suggest they took flip charts and chairs outside to enjoy the sun They thought this was wonderful and left for home with suntans.

My mother's wrist had now totally healed apart from a slight weakness. She was able to do most things but I liked to go to see her as often as I could. She was quite demanding in a passive way and I always felt a tremendous sense of guilt if I missed a couple of days. It was difficult sometimes even to spend time on the telephone.

She lived right in the centre of Mumbles so had very easy access to shops. Although I hated to admit it, she was beginning to get a bit doddery and I was worried about her crossing the road, which was so busy. All the shop keepers knew her – she was such a character – so they all kept an eye on her wanderings.

She did get lonely as she was always 'a people person'. I never mind my own company and love to be alone in my own home. No chance of that at this stage in my life, but, in the past, and hopefully in the future, I would enjoy my solitude again.

Anyway, my mother has always liked people around her and the bustle of a town with plenty of light and traffic noise. She was beginning to get lonely and depressed and would often cry when I got to her flat. She thought her life had been for nothing and she was sad and bitter. I always tried to find the words but not always successfully. She had a lovely flat that everyone envied, enough money to live on and – more or less – her health. I was very concerned about this depression and when I got home I wrote her a letter. Writing it drained me emotionally but I had to do something and if I ignored it, it might be too late.

I told her how much I loved her and how she had influenced my whole life. What a happy childhood I had and how proud I had always been of her. I talked about the things we had laughed at and the places we had walked together. I said it was because of her artistic nature and inventiveness that I had inherited and learnt from her. I could never have achieved what I had without her. She might think she had a sad life but mine had always been happy. I loved John and was happy now. I had everything to thank her for – I owed her my life.

I posted the letter but she couldn't bring herself to speak about it. She was a changed person and seemed more content and happy. She told me later than whenever she started to feel depressed, she would take out her letter and read it.

Chapter Twelve

What a bombshell was about to be dropped!

Lis, who was cooking Sunday lunch had been complaining of an upset tummy and this was lasting over quite a long period off and on. I used to tell her it was just an excuse for a port and brandy – John's magic cure for upset tummies!

Anyway, it was to turn out that she was pregnant! She was as surprised as anyone. She would therefore be finishing work before long and someone else would have to do Sundays.

The time was getting closer and no one was prepared to take it on. Kate was clinging to her Sundays – fair enough. The general feeling, in my absence, was that I should do it. "Lis, how could you do this to me?" There was nothing for it – until we found someone else. The snag with a small business is that you have to be prepared to jump into the breach. I didn't mind the building, the cleaning, waitressing even, but – cooking! It was worse than selling shoes – I hated the thought.

Kate went through it all in detail and said it was easy. Yes, but I still had to do everything else as well. Breakfasts, tables, laundry, flowers. And how would John manage without me out front – he couldn't remember anybody's name without his prompt. No problem, Marcia would take the orders.

O.K. – let's have a go!

I had to cook the breakfasts of course, but at the same time I could get the meats in the oven so that the gravies could be made early. The two girls helping me would come in at nine o'clock. They could get on with the Yorkshire pudding batter and desserts, then once I was finished with the breakfasts, the vegetables could go on to cook and the starters prepared. The root vegetables would have been peeled the night before.

When the breakfast room was empty I could sort the tables for lunch and get it ready for the cleaners. I would have already prepared the second dining room the night before and done the flowers. The laundry was permanently on and whoever was around would fold and put away.

I would also have listed the bookings on the order pad with the tables that were still available marked. This was ready for Marcia when she came in.

Back into the kitchen to do the gravies and about half past eleven, the Yorkshire puddings and roast potatoes went in. I did these in two batches so they would be crisp for the later diners.

The waitresses came in at half past eleven and the potwash at midday, the latter to a huge pile of dirty pans and breakfast dishes. We always had two pot washers on a Sunday.

Usually, the first diners arrived about half past twelve, sometimes earlier if they wanted to enjoy a few drinks. We got to know the people who liked to loiter over drinks before eating so we would delay sending their order through. We didn't want to rush anyone.

Well, I was ready – wasn't I? I had checked and double checked. I was petrified but trying not to show it. Shaking inside. There were sixty-five people booked in. What if I made a mistake. There was one table of twelve – horror! What was I doing? I couldn't possibly get through this. It was Ilfracombe harbour all over again!

I had to get my act together. I went to the bar – put a glass under the whisky optic and pushed up – twice! I could see John's jaw drop

Sunday lunch – Marcia on left

133

but he knew by my face not to utter a word. I never drink whisky, hate it. I threw it back and returned to the kitchen. After a while, my body stopped shaking.

Well, I got through it and when it was all over, I felt I was on a terrific 'high'. Whether it was relief or the whisky, I don't know.

I was tired but still had to do the tables and laundry, although the girls did help me a lot. At this time we were closed Sunday nights. Collapse time!

Another stray cat had been getting nearer and nearer to the kitchen door. What a mess! Thin and matted with runny eyes. A really ugly tortoise shell that surely no one could ever love?

We just had to help it so, of course, she was fed. She was desperate to be loved and we were failing to keep her outside. There was nothing for it but a visit to the Vet. She was in quite a bad way but fairly young. I left the vet's surgery with my purse about thirty pounds lighter and an appointment for her to have a hysterectomy in a few weeks' time when she was stronger,

No one could bear to pick her up or touch her, apart from me, and the general opinion was that she would never amount to much. I called her 'Annwyl' – beloved one! Poor thing.

Well, as the weeks passed by she did blossom into a very pretty little cat. She wasn't clever like Winni but was so affectionate and soon found her way to the most comfortable chair in the drawing room. We had to be careful – it's surprising how many people don't like cats or are allergic to them and Annwyl would seek them all out. We didn't have to worry about Winni jumping onto laps – she didn't need the affection that Annwyl did – she was intelligent and well adjusted.

Celyn was a trained cuddler and would have loved to be a lap dog. It was too much that Annwyl could manage this – a total newcomer!

We were beginning to get more and more non-business people. We had appeared in 'Country Living' magazine. Just a small article but it was most complimentary and portrayed us perfectly. It described the grounds and the countryside and we had quite a good response to this.

Soon afterwards, a feature appeared in the 'Daily Telegraph' with even more detail of how Fairyhill had been 'saved' by us. We couldn't have wished for more if we'd written it ourselves. Spoiling everyone was paying off – you never knew who you were talking to – journalist or inspector!

We found that the majority of these couples were middle aged or retired who didn't want the bright lights and late nights.

Although we always made children very welcome, we did point out to parents when booking, that we were not really geared up for them – no play room, paddling pools, sand-pits, etc. We willingly baby-sat the children that did come while the parents enjoyed a romantic meal. We tried to encourage the parents of young children to feed them early in the conservatory which made for a more relaxed evening all round.

Another big attraction was the fact that we welcomed dogs. We both adore dogs and indeed, all animals, and we reckoned that a lot of people had their holidays in this country because they wouldn't put their beloved pets into kennels. The same people with their dogs were to return year after year. The dogs were no problem at all. They would stay in the car whilst the owners were eating then spend the night in the bedroom. We never had a problem. In fact, a lot less hassle than a spoilt child!

Celyn was the perfect hostess – she seemed to realise that they wouldn't stay too long.

Now our rooms were in use at weekends when 'Full' meant double the people – double the breakfasts.

Sunday mornings were becoming exhausting. Twenty plus for breakfast whilst trying to get on with the lunch. The poor guests were deprived of a lie-in as we just had to have the breakfast room clear in time to lay up for lunch. We did chat to them about it the night before and they were very understanding. Most were walkers and wanted to be off by ten anyway.

Couples staying, often meant afternoon tea and more chatting during the daytime. Quite a lot would go up to their rooms when returning during the afternoon and make tea there. They always had a good supply of tea and coffee which was easier for them – and us. Also, if they had a disturbed night, it was comforting for them to have their own tea making facilities. Everyone had our night number if they required anything but we were very rarely disturbed.

I had been cooking Sunday lunch for about four months. My weekends were often a nightmare, particularly if we had a wedding on a Saturday afternoon. Then Saturday would be an eighteen hour day before an early start on Sunday, cooking breakfasts, then lunch and sometimes, if we had residents on a Sunday night, they had to eat too. Worse than the evening meal was the fact that people liked to have a drink and a chat with us. It was always easier if there were half a dozen people or more as they would all chat together in the drawing room and we could collapse in a chair in the hall. If there was only one couple, we felt we wanted to entertain them. They didn't want to be on their own – they might as well stay at home.

We desperately needed a couple of weeks off and it was during this period that we had the offer of a villa in Corfu. It was so tempting and we thought we could manage eight days away with a few free days at home. Kate said she would manage and her parents would come in to help too.

We left on a Friday and it was bliss. My main pleasure was on the Sunday when I could visualise the pressure in the kitchen and was so grateful to be out of it for a couple of weeks.

We really enjoyed the rest and arrived back at Fairyhill about half past eight on the following Saturday when everything was in full swing. We were hoping to take our things upstairs and unwind slowly for a couple of days more. That was pie in the sky!

That day's laundry was piled high on the floor in the potwash. No one had done it. I had to get it on to wash so there would be enough sheets and napkins for the morning and so that the machines would be ready for the evening's cloths and napkins. Had anyone organised the tables for lunch? Kate said she hadn't and she was leaving early that night. On going through the door she said "You're cooking breakfast and lunch tomorrow, I'm off for two days!"

I couldn't believe that this could be happening. Was it my fault? Hadn't I made it clear we were off for longer? Maybe not but surely, no one should be expected to do this.

I was up most of the night catching up and checking everything for the next day. This was much worse than if I hadn't been away. It was four days before I eventually unpacked, on the Wednesday. The next holiday we had I would make sure that we closed. We had to wait another three years for this.

Val in the office came in one morning and we knew instantly that something was on her mind. She told us that she had been offered a job she really wanted to take. She loved it with us but this other offer supplied a car and she would be travelling all over the country. We would be very sorry to lose her but it couldn't be helped. I hated change of staff. We all got along so well and anyone new not only had to be good at their job but had to fit in with everyone else and, most important of all, have a sense of humour.

Well, true to form, Marcia had a friend living near her in Landimore who could do the job. This was good enough for us. So Marian arrived and spent a week or two sitting in with Val.

Marian was extremely quiet and reserved and we wondered what she would be like with the guests. She was also very subdued when answering the telephone. John soon took her in hand. "Don't just say 'hullo' Marian – smile when you answer even though they can't see you, and almost sing, 'Good morning, Fairyhill'. You must always remember that you are our link with the world and your voice is Fairyhill. People will judge us by the way you sound."

She took to it like a duck to water and in addition, kept all our paper work and bookings in order. She fitted in well around the kitchen table for coffee and chats. She would bring the reservations book through with her so we could take any calls in the kitchen. Celyn was left 'on duty' for twenty minutes while we all caught up on any gossip.

Two months after Val left, Marcia was offered a very good full time job with a building society. She was sorry to leave us but her husband had been made redundant and she needed the extra money. My first thoughts were 'Who was going to take the orders Sunday lunchtimes?

By now Marcia knew all our regulars by name and they all liked her. She promised that she would continue working just for the lunchtime twelve thirty until two o'clock. Then I had to leave the kitchen, shower, change and come out front with John.

We bought all our fruit and vegetables from Colin Jones in Sketty. Sometimes we would get new season vegetables from the local farmers but mainly we telephoned our order to Colin every morning and it would be delivered soon after lunch.

All our herbs and more exotic produce we had from Vin Sullivan in Abergavenny, a wonderful family firm who could never do enough to help. They delivered three times a week, or even overnight if we were desperate.

Colin Jones told us one morning that he had a pumpkin we could have. He said he couldn't sell it. He brought it down and now we could see why it was unsaleable. It was huge and had won first prize in the local agricultural show. It weighed half a hundredweight! Kate stared at it saying, "What am I supposed to do with that?"

Next thing we knew, John appeared, laughing, with the chain saw, "Stand back". We were all helpless, while he proceeded to cut it into manageable pieces.

We had pumpkin as a vegetable, pumpkin soup and pumpkin pie. We froze gallons of soup and after giving to anyone who could bear it, we had to throw the remainder away.

Jennifer, who had been doing Monday nights instead of Kate now announced that she was leaving. This was serious. Who would do Mondays now? No volunteers. Stale mate. Eventually, from Kate,

"You could do it Midgie." It was always 'Midgie' when wheedling!

"Are you serious, Kate? I'm no chef."

Kate: "Yes you could, if I showed you everything, and prepared the sauces."

The only comment from John was, "You can do it, Babe," a phrase I was hearing quite a lot.

Needless to say, Babe did it. In addition to Sundays.

Our second Christmas season was approaching and we were busier than ever with private parties, We were having a lot of requests for residential bookings for Christmas but we decided against this. We had learnt from last year that Christmas Eve was quiet – no one went out to eat in the evening, so it was better for us to close and use the time preparing for the next day. We didn't want residents who would have to be entertained Christmas Eve, Christmas morning and Boxing Day. I didn't care how much they were prepared to pay, Boxing Day was our precious day off!

I went through all the decorating bit again and the same procedure for Christmas Day. We had a lot of the same people as last year and it was equally successful.

We didn't bother with our sit down dinner – everyone preferred to get home. I think we had a sandwich but just managed to microwave a plated up Christmas meal the next day. What bliss, to lock the doors and have our home back – even if it was only one day!

In five days, we would be having another big night – New Year's Eve. This was an equally big success. Again, with a delicious set seven course meal but this night, of course, we had a lot of residents. We usually succeeded in getting most people into the drawing room for midnight to top up all of them with champagne. Everyone enjoyed it, including the staff and no one seemed to stay later than one o'clock, which was a bonus.

1987 and Lis had, by this time, had her baby and was starting to do the odd stint of waitresses. I had been doing lunches for about six months. I was almost afraid to broach the subject! Would she take over from me ... PLEASE?

She wouldn't mind but the snag was that Andrew couldn't cope with the baby all morning and if she had to pay a baby minder it wouldn't be worth her while. Well, it would be worth my while – "I'll pay for a baby minder, Lis, just come back!" I pleaded.

Thank goodness, she agreed and I could hardly believe it – I was free of lunches. Now, I just had Monday nights and the hundred and one other things to see to, but I was so happy. Looking back on those six months, I marvel at how I ever survived it! Worse was to come.

Chapter Thirteen

Now that Val had left, John had to be in the office to hand out bills in the morning. Although we had Marian, she couldn't come in as early as Val because she had children to get off to school. Her hours were nine o'clock until five.

In between serving breakfasts, John had to rush down to the hall when Celyn barked, see to the bills and farewells then rush back to continue serving. It did get a bit hairy at times and it was always a relief to see Marian coming through the kitchen door.

She, like Marcia, used to walk to work. She would arrive in her shorts and walking shoes (or tracksuit and wellies) and change in the staff room before going through to the office. Some busy mornings I would shout to her from the stove, "Quick Marian, go as you are – he's desperate!"

Marian always had her lunch, which was normally just fruit, in the staffroom watching 'Neighbours'. I would very often join her and it was quite pleasant. Sometimes, the cleaning girls would come in and have a sandwich rather than going home. Fairyhill was more a way of life than a job!

Some afternoons when her work had slackened, Marian would come out to the kitchen and help with desserts. She became a champion of the hazelnut meringue!

For quite some time I had been eating so erratically that I decided to take myself in hand. I often went for hours without food if we were really busy and then grab a piece of cheesecake at the end of the night. No good at all.

I decided to go on a proper sensible eating diet and wrote it all out meticulously. Not content with this, I had to get everyone else on it. A few of our girls were over weight and I bullied them into agreeing. I certainly wasn't what one could call a strict employer, far from it, we all worked together, but they felt they ought to humour me over this.

They were all weighed and everyone charted. They had a list of meals for the whole week plus a routine of exercises. I would insist every morning, that the cleaning girls spent five minutes in the conference room rolling on the floor – for the hips and bottom. I watched them so they couldn't cheat. It was a riot! I cross examined them whenever they were in and at the end of the week they were weighed. It created a lot of enthusiasm and we all did well. Kate didn't want to get involved with this as it would have meant giving up her nightly 'unwinding' gin and tonics, but nearly everyone else was totally engrossed. It went on for quite a few months until it gradually died a natural death. We all felt better for it.

If we could possibly manage it, John and I would always sit in the restaurant once everyone else was seated. We wouldn't eat a meal but perhaps a starter or some cheese with a couple of glasses of wine. People liked to see us sitting there and we could soon get a general conversation going especially if there were just a few tables of two. On these quiet evenings we really enjoyed ourselves. It was better than a dinner party – I didn't have to cook or clear up. On these occasions Celyn would feel it was alright to come in and with her and Winni in front of the fire, people really felt relaxed.

Some evenings were really stimulating. I remember one in particular – the conversational topics were wide and varied. Later, when it came around to the respective professions, it transpired that four of them were High Court judges. One American, one Australian and the other two British. Quite amazing.

On busier nights we would still go in to sit but, of course, we would be up and down more, seeing to bills and chatting. We could always keep a close eye on what was happening in the restaurant and could quickly intervene in any mistake or problem.

People were mostly relaxed before getting to the dining room so were happy and receptive to anything they were served. If the food happened to be good, which it was, then this was a bonus.

We were always congratulated on our desserts. These were set out on our old refectory table in the middle of the billiard room and people would gasp on entering. It was laden with a variety of goodies: cheesecake, banoffee pie, Queen of puddings, Pavlova, Hazelnut meringue, Trifle, Bread and butter pudding, Fresh fruit salad, Gateau and a cheeseboard. Kate was also making the most wonderful ice cream.

I made and tried to introduce Port jelly for the not so sweet toothed. I also made elderflower jelly from my homemade elderflower wine. I set this in a shallow tin to a depth of half an inch then cut into cubes. These I broke up and filled a wine glass where they sparkled like cut jewels. I loved these but not many people risked them – too tempted by the 'goodies'.

This display was described in one of the food guides as 'a groaning Billy Bunter table.' Many people came just for the desserts.

We often tried to remove one in place of a new experiment but it was always someone's favourite that had been removed, so we gave up and stuck to the old faithfuls.

We had done a few marquee weddings in our first summer, which I found quite stressful. I always felt 'out of control' with a large number of people, although they look after themselves better than a small group. I was concerned that these weddings would interfere with our diners and residents and vice versa. I had this awful horror of upsetting people.

The next year we were approached by two separate friends who wanted their daughters' weddings at Fairyhill. They were both large weddings – about two hundred guests, and we didn't want to refuse.

We hired the marquees from a nice man in Abergavenny who also supplied round tables and chairs. All we had to do was tell him the size required. We also had a smaller 'service' tent at the side for stacking dirty dishes before taking them through to the kitchen. We had there two old chest freezers lined with ice then filled with bottles of white wine and champagne, topped up with lots more ice. This worked brilliantly and kept everything cold for longer than needed.

The marquee was erected on the Thursday which left me all day Friday to sort things out. We would have hired crockery, cutlery and glasses for this amount of people.

Kate always did wonderful buffets which looked spectacular. They were more work than a hot meal but less formal and most people preferred them. On these occasions her father always came in to do the carving of cold meats. He was a keen amateur cook and she was always glad of his moral and practical support.

Digressing slightly, I remember on one occasion, we had been sent a frozen turkey instead of fresh. It was too late to change and we panicked about defrosting it. I filled our bath with cold water and dropped the turkey in. John nearly had heart failure on entering the bathroom to see this 'body' floating upside down with it's legs splayed out! Everything turned out well and by the time it was stuffed and cooked, it was delicious.

We had everything organised even down to the Portaloos and the day duly dawned. On both occasions – torrential rain from dawn, right through!

Instead of welcoming drinks being served outside in the sunshine, we were fighting to carry trays of champagne through the throng that was packed into the drawing room, halls and spreading into the dining room. No one could move.

Most of the bride's family at the second wedding lived away and were staying overnight with us. All the surnames were 'Walters' and in the confusion, someone, who had not previously booked, was occupying a room. When the rightful 'Walters' turned up, we didn't have a room for him. All this on a Saturday afternoon when Marian was at home! Amidst all the mayhem I dashed upstairs to prepare our guest room and, full of apologies, took him there, free of charge of course.

I was almost wreckage by the time they went in to eat!

The waitresses had to travel from the kitchen, through the conservatory then over ten yards of open ground to the service tent. Although we put matting here over the lawn, it was soon muddy and they were very wet.

By the evening, the rain had come down the outside walls of the marquee and seeped underneath. Consequently, the serving area behind the bar was a quagmire! We had to buy three of the staff new shoes.

The guests were oblivious to what we were all suffering and had a great time, thank goodness.

John was out of action for most of the night as one guest had parked his car in the road and everyone else had parked behind, thus eventually blocking the whole road. He had to find each driver in turn, starting at the end car and gradually clear the congestion. It took hours and hours!

The last of our girls left about half past two in the morning after helping with all laundry and as much washing up as we could manage. There were only glasses left for the morning.

I remember being so tired, I could hardly walk. About half past three, while carrying something through the kitchen to the potwash, I slipped and fell. I didn't hurt myself physically, but sat there and burst into tears. I felt so sorry for myself – I didn't deserve this!

Chapter Fourteen

We now decided to think about the Stable, and I began to draw up plans. Our builders had long since left us, having worked on Fairyhill for two and a half years. Martin's wife had had two children in that time and Mark had married and produced one child. Now we had to find other builders.

We had already put on a new roof and made the doorway bigger so that John could drive in on the tractor. It still housed some logs so the first thing to do was transport these around to the wood shed in the big walled garden. Once it was empty, I could sit in a corner quietly and let my imagination do the rest.

I had always wanted a gallery and there was enough height for this. We would have to install a spiral staircase, which I don't really like, and this would lead on to the pine-end gallery which would

Walled garden showing rear of Stable

Same view with Winni, Midge and Celyn with mum in doorway

then continue around the whole length of the building. There would be two bedrooms en suite leading off. The smaller bedroom would be above the kitchen which would be walled off from the main room.

I wanted all the doors semi-arched to a point and I envisaged looking through the kitchen door at a spotlighted dresser. Underneath the gallery would be the 'monstrosity' also lit by a concealed light. The windows would also be arched and the main room would be dark and church like with lots of lamps.

There is a wonderful high-walled secret garden behind the stable and we would build on into this, the second bedroom above a large garden room.

I could see it all quite clearly and drew it absolutely to scale on my trusty graph paper and eventually on a much larger plan.

We now had to get an architect to transpose my plans for planning and building purposes. I got the same sympathetic architect that had got planning permission for our bathrooms and he was really excited about my ideas. I thought all would be plain sailing.

Unfortunately, he must have passed it on to someone else in his office and when the plans came back for approval, they were totally altered. I returned them with several comments and they tried again.

"Monstrosity" under gallery in stable

This time the gallery went completely around the building with the stairs in a different place. A third lot were submitted with supporting pillars holding up the gallery. As for my garden room with its wooden arches all around, this had changed to awful modern patio doors!

I was really cross and insisted they came down. I never saw my original man again and the one who came was on a totally different plane. He said the gallery had to be supported or it would fall down and the bedroom above the sun room couldn't be supported by a wooden structure!

He was more than a little sheepish when I suggested the whole frame of the sunroom could be steel, clad with wood and the gallery could again be a steel continuation of the bedroom floors. It really only needs a bit of common sense, which, incidentally, should be renamed 'rare sense'.

We eventually won a Design Award for the Stable and I'm afraid I did not acknowledge the architects' part in it at all. I think we did it in spite of them!

The next thing was to find some responsible builders who could also understand what I wanted. Derek Heard from Pontardulais eventually started with his two sons and about three men. We got on quite well and they did a top class job with fine workmanship. Derek was a bit of a chatterbox and as I was trying to run an hotel as well, I often had to fight to make sure he had my point. "Are you listening to me Derek?" He would laugh then. I was constantly behind them to make sure they knew the next step. I'm sure they hated to see me approaching.

John might have spotted something but wouldn't tell them. He would call me to do the dirty work. I hated it too, when something was wrong and really had to pluck up all my courage to tell them it had to be altered.

They were fine generally, but anything I wanted that was slightly out of the ordinary, "Can't be done, Midge." I would ask to have the reason explained and we usually got around it. What they meant was that they had never done anything like it before!

We wanted very thick, big doors – the same both sides – no latch and brace. "Can't be done," said Derek. He hadn't really recovered from the arched shape of the doorways yet! I suggested they clad over the latch and brace, so making the door the same on both sides – and thick!

Inside original stable

Same view

We found a holly tree down in the woods which had been dead for years. It would be perfect to form a mantelpiece behind the woodstove on top of a stone wall. It was rough and undulating and just what we wanted. We brought it up and left it in the stable until they were ready to use it. I was just in time one day to stop Derek taking it up the saw mill "to have it squared off." I paled!

When I said that I wanted it left rounded with the bark on, he was incredulous. He said that unless it was at least flat on the bottom it couldn't rest on the stonework. I asked very diplomatically, if he thought it possible to suspend the tree on brackets fixed firmly into the wall and then perhaps build the stonework up to it. He thought about it and they all had a discussion.

This is what they eventually did and we were all very pleased with the result. They tolerated me well and were very patient.

The whole house worked out exactly as I had visualised. Now we had to bring the big dresser that was in the house kitchen over to the Stable kitchen. I had made sure that the ceiling had been put in the exact height to take it. I could now sit in the main room and look through my arched doorway at the dresser. People have said I'm clever, but I think you can either visualise the finished result or you can't, and being clever doesn't really enter into it.

My mother could do this and I remember her saying "Wherever you sit in a room, make sure every viewpoint is a picture." I think, ideally, you need corners and alcoves – a square or oblong room can be very boring.

We had a small dresser in the Coach House so we brought that over to the house kitchen to replace the big one that had gone to the Stable. It didn't look as impressive but we soon got used to it. We had to buy a sideboard for the drawing room to replace the 'monstrosity'. It was a matter of borrowing from Peter to pay Paul!

Of course, we had to buy a lot of bits and pieces – tapestries, pictures and lots of brassy things, as well as furniture. We went to the Cotswolds for most of these. We had found in Stow-on-the-Wold the most enormous central light fitting that was perfect. It cost a fortune but we really had to have something that big on a huge chain, to look right. It hung level with the gallery and we couldn't have found anything better. The builders had put a big extra beam in the roof to hold it and it took three men on scaffolding to fix it.

We fitted the two bedrooms out with televisions, telephone and tea making facilities so now we had two extra rooms or a de-luxe suite. We could also use it for self-catering. It was eventually to be our home if and whenever we sold Fairyhill, and it was very special.

Although the conservatory was very light and attractive, on a sunny day, be it summer or winter, it was far too glaring and needed some shade.

I had a brilliant idea of nailing wooden trellis inside the sloping glass roof and then threading through a mass of artificial vines. I wanted to darken the trellis before fixing it, so very quickly, sloshed it over with dark creosote. Having done this, up it went and within a couple of hours the greenery was in place. Exactly right – lovely, mottled shade with a cool, relaxed feel.

The next night the conservatory was full. The evening was cool so we had lit the woodstove. Halfway through the evening I went to see if anything was needed and there was this terrible smell. After a while my eyes started to burn. The creosote fumes were overpowering! No one had said anything but I just had to mention it. Yes, they could smell it and yes – their eyes were burning! They didn't seem unduly upset but I bought everyone a liqueur and deleted their drinks and wine from the bills. What an idiot I was. It took weeks to wear off!

Had we realised at the start that we would be so busy, we would have trebled the size of the conservatory and joined it up with the billiard room. It could easily have been done, with big French doors closed off if necessary then our three dining rooms would be linked. Perhaps we would do it sometime in the future.

Lis didn't really want to work every Sunday so I suggested to Kate that we advertise for a full time second chef. There was absolutely no way that I was going back in that kitchen on Sundays – I was already doing Monday nights.

We were lucky in finding Julie, who was only twenty-one but very capable and sensible. She did not live locally but had to drive in all the way from Pontardawe, twenty-five miles. We paid travelling expenses so it wouldn't affect her wages. She had worked in a busy restaurant before and quickly picked up what Kate had to teach her. She was soon able to relieve me of Mondays and take turns with Lis. I felt as though a weight had been lifted from me.

Julie was great and was to stay with us for six years.

Annwyl was proving to be quite a hunter. One evening, she walked through the French doors in the drawing room, along the hall and into the kitchen carrying a baby rabbit in her mouth. On

Kate, Jane and Julie

reaching the kitchen, she dropped it and the poor thing ran off. Pandemonium. We were all chasing it around, including a few guests who had come to see what all the noise was about. It went behind the stove. Kate climbed up and stuck a broom down the back. It eventually ran out when one of our guests threw his coat over it. I took it outside and put it into the bushes. The poor thing was shivering so much, I doubt if it survived.

Another evening, one of the waitresses was serving a table of six people in the billiard room when she thought she had stepped on a lady's handbag. On looking down, she saw half a squirrel! Where was the other half? She didn't know what to do so, kicked it further under the table and hoped for the best!

One really amazing thing that Annwyl accomplished was to bring five baby ducklings all the way from the lake, which is about one hundred and fifty yards away, through the cat flap, through the kitchen and up the back stairs to be placed on the landing outside our room. She must have made five separate trips, to bring them, one at a time. They were all alive and we heard them cheeping when we woke. It was hard to believe that they had survived the ordeal. John found a shoe box, popped them in and carried them back to the lake. In they went and swam off, none the worse for their adventure. I only hope they found the mother duck.

This was becoming more like Whipsnade rather than a smart, elegant restaurant. Emily was still around and often did a quick circuit of one of the rooms. Nine times out of ten no one noticed – she was so quick and quiet. I would make pacifying comments – "Things like this happen in the country – it's only Emily." Once, I heard a lady say, "I live in the country but I don't have bats flying around my dining room!"

We still had our set price menu. I was always amazed at the quantity of food people ate and sometimes was wicked enough to think that they had all the courses because they were included in the price. I also wondered if it would be more flexible to price each item individually. In that way, a starter or dessert could be skipped, if required. Perhaps, some people, with a smaller appetite would prefer to have two starters only, or a starter and a pudding. This could apply to older people or residents who didn't want a three course meal every night. Some took advantage of this but not as many as I thought.

We didn't alter the structure of the menu – just wrote prices alongside each item. It didn't seem to deter people from going through it all and it was much better for us as we could be more accurate on our costings.

During this summer of 1987 we were able to get extra casual help from students. We had a lovely French girl called Valerie who had a very pleasant nature and charmed all our guests. She was a friend of Kate and stayed with us all the summer.

Vicky was also young and gorgeous – a real latin beauty. Her family had bought June's old house so she was really close to work. She mostly worked through the holidays but was near enough to fill in other times if we were desperate.

Sue Glover, who also lived only half a mile away and was very quiet initially, turned out to be quite a character. These three girls would waitress, clean or potwash, whatever was required.

We were having a lot of requests for cream teas so I made a sign advertising them and put this out by the gates. Sue took over the teas every afternoon and managed brilliantly. She was sometimes run off her feet and Marian and I had to pitch in. Kate would have made scones so we just had to warm them in the oven.

Terry's wife had approached me with a view to cleaning. We took her on for a while but it didn't work out. She was a Jehovah's Witness and wanted to spread her convictions. The first I learned of this was when I asked young Sue why she was working with her Walkman earphones on. She said, "So that I can't hear Ann!"

Autumn was approaching and we decided to have a third full timer in the kitchen, then we wouldn't be relying on our part time girls so much. We again advertised and once more we were lucky. This was yet another Julie who we decided to call 'Jay'. Jay was about the same age as Julie and was also quite experienced and had been in charge of a busy kitchen. She was a 'homely' girl and her ambition was to marry and have lots of children. I hoped it wouldn't be for a while! They settled in together fairly quickly and were to become close friends.

Now I was absolutely guaranteed to be free of the kitchen forever. Jay and Julie would take it in turns to be in charge when Kate was off and would share Sundays with Lis.

Chapter Fifteen

Although two of our attic rooms were small, we had decided to put double beds into them and charge single room prices. Now that we were so busy, many people were glad of a smaller room at a reasonable price. We also put two bunk beds into the 'boxroom' next door so that any children could stay for the price of breakfast.

Gower in the summer cannot cope as there are not enough hotels. Many have been turned into Rest Homes and Nursing Homes and if people arrive on the off chance, not having previously booked in, they find themselves with nowhere to stay.

For this reason, we kept a list of good Bed and Breakfast accommodation that we personally vetted and when we were full John would ring around to book in people who had called. He would keep trying until he succeeded. This would sometimes continue up to ten o'clock at night – Fridays were the worst, after a good weather forecast! I don't think he ever turned anyone away without finding them a bed.

He was always conscientious and considerate and would spend ages planning excursions and routes for people, very often lending a car. He would drive them himself if they wanted a long walk, having first left their own car at their destination, so they wouldn't have to retrace their steps. Nothing was ever too much trouble for John. As he was in the shop – everyone had to be happy. He took pleasure in guiding them around Wales and booking ahead into the lovely Welsh Rarebit hotels. I know that many foreign visitors – as well as British – left thinking how lovely the Welsh were!

We had so many letters from people expressing their appreciation and yet, we were only doing what anyone would do for their personal guests at home.

Following John's example, Marian and all our other staff were equally helpful and hospitable. We used to tell them, if they were doing the job they might as well look as though they were enjoying it. People were nicer in a pleasant atmosphere.

We did have some very rude and bad-tempered people but the same thing applied. Maybe they had had a worrying day, then perhaps the drive on the motorway was a nightmare and, more likely than not, they'd had trouble finding us. We would apologetically take them to their room and be waiting with a welcome drink when they came down. Celyn would be wagging her tail and by the time they got to the dining room where the girls would be smiling a welcome, they had usually mellowed, and were in a receptive mood for Kate's lovely food.

I came totally unstuck and disillusioned with this practice one day. There was a very miserable couple booked in for dinner and we had failed totally to get a response from them. After the meal they had gone into the drawing room to sit on their own and I sent Celyn in. After a while, I went in smiling and asked if they would like some more coffee. The man beckoned to me. He said he would like to apologise and he thought we deserved some sort of explanation. Everything had been lovely and we were all so friendly, but they had, that afternoon buried their five year old daughter after a riding accident.

It upset me so much. Why hadn't I read the situation better? I felt dreadful and vowed I would tread more carefully in the future.

It was always a thrill when we had someone famous staying. Very often they would have booked under another name and would also look so different. John would never recognise anyone – he was hopeless on names – but I would, and if I missed them, one of the waitresses would pick them out, especially the pop stars. I would recognise the older ones like Donovan and Paul Jones!

Lynne Perrie and her husband stayed one Sunday night and were our only guests. The name didn't mean anything to us and they were late arriving. Here was someone that John did recognise and he was so proud of himself. He whispered to me "It's Ivy from Coronation Street" and then proceeded to call them Mr. and Mrs. Brennan all night! This of course was also her character's name in the 'soap'.

We had a BBC film crew booked in with David Attenborough but unfortunately he wouldn't be arriving until two o'clock in the morning. Normally, John and I always tossed a coin to see who would have to wait up for late arrivals but in this case I offered instantly to wait for one of my favourite people. I stayed curled up in the chair in front of the woodstove until half past two when the taxi arrived. I opened the door and there he was! He apologised profusely, in his charming manner when he saw that Celyn and I had been waiting. I was quite tongue tied and the only thing I could come out with was "It's a pleasure."

It was strange that within a couple of weeks we had another film crew accompanying David Bellamy with his wife and children. I don't know how the subject cropped up but it appeared that they were having difficulty in finding Siamese kittens in London. I made a couple of phone calls and eventually sent them off to an address in Caswell. They were very pleased with the service!

It was 1988 and we had now been open for three years. The time seemed to be flying by and one day merged into the next. The general daily routine was more or less the same but with some days more hectic.

Occasionally, in the quieter winter months, or whenever we could manage it, John and I would drive off for the day. It would be a last minute decison and only when we had early breakfasts and no last minute delays. We prepared everything ready for the evening first and checked that the girls were alright, then John would always said, "Quick – let's go while the going's good!"

He had a BMW M3 which he hardly ever had the chance to use. It was his pride and joy and he loved driving it. We would go up to the Cotswolds for a pub lunch and a leisurely stroll around. The wonderful feeling we had driving down Fairyhill lane. One of us would always say "Can you believe we are actually out?"

We enjoyed every minute of these stolen few hours. To be just the two of us again – totally alone. This short time was enough to re-vitalise us. We were always back by five o'clock before Marian left to catch up with any news. We never knew what might have been planned for that evening – the number of diners might have trebled in the time we'd been away and we had to allow ourselves plenty of time to prepare. I have never been able to leave things to chance and 'hope for the best.'

Although we were very busy, it was a good time. I never really minded having lost my social life. Wasn't the world coming to me? I only saw my friends if they came to eat, and then I wasn't relaxed enough to spend time chatting to them. It was almost like living a totally false existence. Very pleasant, but cocooned against the everyday drab world outside. I didn't really know what was happening generally out there. I didn't read newspapers and there wasn't time for television, except the occasional Sunday night. Even then, I usually fell asleep. I sometimes recorded programmes if I managed to remember, and would watch for half an hour before going to bed – just to unwind. Most nights, I must admit, I was already pretty well unwound – or unravelled!

We had early mornings and late nights but at least we lived 'over the shop' and didn't have to travel to get to work. We could disappear in turns for the odd half hour if things were quiet and still be on hand for any emergency. John and I often went all day without bumping into one another and never really had time to ourselves. Tensions never could progress to arguments. We could never have a row as there was always an audience. Surrounded by staff or guests it would have been impossible. We had no private life at all.

In spite of all this, it was very exhilarating. People are so interesting and we never knew who would come through the door. We already knew that one can never judge by appearances and the scruffiest tramp could well turn out to be one of the aristocracy. Generally, we found that the higher up the social scale, the more down to earth and appreciative people were.

We were past the age to be impressed by the 'nouveau riche'. We had far more pleasure relaxing the more humble groups who had, perhaps, saved up to come to Fairyhill for a special occasion. They would arrive a little in awe and afraid that it would all be too 'posh'. It was a bigger feather in our cap to send them away having enjoyed every minute of their visit and looking forward to the next.

Sheila, one of our general factotums was moving on, which would leave a big gap. Not only did she waitress but was also on the cleaning rota. Bringing three boys up alone was hard but she was doing it well. She had been taking a commercial course in addition to working with us and now had the chance of a good job. Luckily, two of her sons were still available for potwashing.

Pat came as a waitress to replace Sheila and had worked with Kate in the past. Pat was very efficient and was always cheerful. She was the busiest person I have every met and had about four jobs. Cleaning in the mornings, school dinners lunchtimes and waitressing or bar work at night. We had to give her 'set' nights so that she could fit around her other jobs. Tuesdays, Fridays, Saturdays and Sunday lunchtimes Pat would be with us. Sometimes she arrived on a Saturday night straight from waitressing at a wedding in another hotel. Very often, her young daughter, Sian would accompany her. Sian would have been about seven years old then and would watch TV in the staff room or amuse herself with something she brought with her. As she got older Sian was reluctantly persuaded to 'chop something' or carry dishes. It was such a waste to see anyone sitting around doing nothing, whatever their age!

Lynne knocked on our door one day asking about work in the kitchen. Lynne lived in Llangennith, two miles away and hadn't worked since her son had been born about sixteen years previously. We didn't need anyone in the kitchen so she said she would waitress. "No" she had never done that before either. She was buxom and cheerful and Kate and I liked the look of her so said we'd give her a try.

Lis, who also lived in Llangennith, thought it hilarious that Lynne should work at Fairyhill. When we asked the reason, she said "Well, Lynne is great and a real tonic, but I can't see her fitting in here – she's so feather-brained and dramatic."

On her first night we decided to put her with Valerie, the French girl, who knew exactly what to do and would teach her well.

The first shock when she arrived was the flowing, fringed, purple sash over the voluminous black skirt. The sash could be remedied but there was nothing we could do about the black bra showing through the white blouse! My bras wouldn't have done the job at all!

Lynne was not 'born to the job' and had to be chivvied along. She was more interested in having a chat with everyone. She and Valerie got on well and there was always a lot of giggling. Lynne was never to become our most efficient waitress but she was such a warm person and always put the guests well-being first. She remembered everyones name and knew what they liked or didn't like. It was a new life for her and she loved the excitement of the restaurant.

There was to be even more laughter now that Lynne was aboard!

June was also about to leave us. She and her husband had bought Dane's Dyke', a pub in Llanmadoc, so she was off. I had been trying to persuade her into the kitchen over the years but she wasn't interested. Now, she regretted it as, hopefully, she would be doing meals in the pub and could have picked up a lot of tips from us.

I remember her last day with us. She had been working in the morning and was also on the potwash rota for that evening. It was a Saturday and she and her husband had been celebrating throughout the afternoon in the 'Greyhound'. Consequently, she was in no fit state to work when she arrived with us at six o'clock. She insisted on staying nevertheless. She was really funny and just wanted to stay in the kitchen chatting. Kate had to keep sending her out. "Get back to that sink, June." On one of her staggering trips back through the kitchen, she seemed more unsteady than usual. As she came through from the potwash, she had inadvertently stepped into Celyn's water bowl, which was now stuck fast onto her shoe. It was so funny. She hadn't even noticed, but all work came to a standstill until everyone had stopped laughing! I could hear them from the bar and came to see what was happening.

Kate had such a terribly loud laugh and we made such a noise that we always felt obliged to tell our diners when we had these laughing jags, what was happening. It helped to explain any delays caused by these hysterical outbursts, and it also amused them and made them feel part of the family!

Because we had lost both Sheila and June our cleaning rota was suffering. We only had Diane as a regular with a few who would come occasionally. This wasn't very satisfactory and it often meant Diane coming more often than she really wanted. She had a busy life feeding husband and son who were farmers and expected four cooked meals a day.

Gill was yet another from Llangennith and like Lynne, was full of fun. She was rough and ready and swore like a trooper. She managed to control this most of the time but it did occasionally slip out. She had such a lovely nature that no one really minded, that was just Gill.

Vera also started about this time and was the complete opposite to Gill. Vera was a 'born again' Christian, and very serious. She did laugh sometimes and it totally transformed her face but this didn't happen often enough. She appeared to treat her work as a penance whereas the rest of the girls seemed to enjoy it. She was very conscientious and was ready to take all the hours that were available. She would work every day if she possibly could and also waitress whenever needed. She was a very private person and I never really knew what she was thinking. I could rely completely on Vera – she was always ready to step in whenever and if ever we were desperate. She was the most efficient of all our girls – I just wished that she would smile more!

Despite the seriousness of Vera, she eventually blended in with the rest of the girls who, nevertheless, watched their 'P's and Q's' – especially Gill!

Lynne took Vera under her wing and for two such opposites, they got on very well. I suspect that Vera thought Lynne not professional enough but what she lacked in formality she made up for in personality. I know Lynne became extremely fond of Vera and always stood up for her.

We had increased our seating capacity by putting 'emergency' tables at various places. Two were in the conservatory which meant we could seat sixteen in there. By moving the sideboard out of the dining room into the hall we could seat twenty-four with thirty-five in the billiard room. We could also seat up to twenty in the conference room. It all depended on table sizes but it was possible to seat a maximum of ninety-five.

John couldn't bear to turn anyone away having worked so hard to get them there. However many times I would say, "O.K. John, we're full now," he would keep taking the bookings. I hated double bookings and only agreed to them lunchtimes when the later table was aware that there might be a delay.

Of course, he did know that he couldn't do it on the standard busy times, Mothers' Day, bank holidays, Christmas and New Year but, Sunday lunches were fair game to John. He would accept the booking then leave it to me to get them in!

Kate would relay through to me, "Tell him to stop, will you – we're out of potatoes" The message would be returned, "Send one of the potwash boys to buy more." John would be smiling and serving in the bar and be oblivious to the panic 'backstage'.

There was no such thing as 'Full' to John.

As I have said, Kate's pudding table was a joy to behold and it almost put people off their main course, worrying whether their favourite dessert would still be available by the time they were ready. We usually had a clutch of various plated-up desserts in the fridge that had been previously booked 'just in case'.

One of our emergency tables was situated at the end of the pudding table and this particular lady, who was rather grand and on her second visit, was watching the Amaretto cheesecake disappearing before her eyes. There was one portion left on the plate when she called me over. In the middle of telling me her fears, she turned back to the table and exclaimed, "Oh my Gawd – it's gawn!" I explained to her that we did have another cheesecake so she could relax – all was well. I there and then saw that Lynne reserved her a piece and, knowing Lynne, it would have been extra large to make amends!

Many people found it difficult to decide which dessert to chose. We would often give them a variety. Some wouldn't budge from their favourite, so we just put a small sample of another in addition.

If I ever opened another restaurant, I would be very tempted to do starters and puds only – forget the main course!

I was very possessive about the Stable and loath to let anyone stay in it. I was improving as time passed but only showed it to people I thought would enjoy it. It had such a wonderful 'feel' and I always felt at peace there. Maybe because it was my brain-child – it had all come out of my head and 'happened'. If I had a spare half hour I would disappear there and lie in the walled garden where I was hidden from everyone. I only told Marian where I was in case of emergencies. Although it was quite close to the main house, it could have been in the depths of nowhere. Everyone that stayed there felt the same tranquillity.

My mother thought it beautiful. Although she didn't really like the country – "It's too quiet and too dark"; she said she felt 'safe' in the Stable. Its walls were three feet thick and there was protection physically and emotionally. Whenever she came down we would go over to sit, depending on whether anyone was staying there, of course.

Anthea now came to join the cleaning rota. Her sister had been with us for a short time but that hadn't worked out. Anthea lived in Crofty and had one son and twin girls. Simon was about ten and the twins six. We often found during school holidays that the staff room would be full of children. They would come in with the various mums and more often than not, play outside in the grounds. But if wet, there was always television. I was pleased that they all felt happy enough in their jobs to do this. The children seemed to enjoy it too.

Anthea's twins were always anxious for jobs. They would be issued with dusters and polish or could be found carrying linen or other requisites up to the rooms. They were wonderful on brasses and would sit at the kitchen table for hours rubbing away and chatting.

Anthea was also very reliable and conscientious with masses of common sense and was more than capable of seeing the funny side of things. This was just as well when she was on the same shift as Gill!

Marilyn started the same time as Anthea and they lived next door to each other. She could work only at certain times and then brought her little boy, Craig with her. It seemed that sometimes there were more children than staff!

In addition to the cleaning, the morning girls would also do the vegetables for the evening. This could take a couple of hours and Anthea's twins would enjoy peeling and chopping carrots or any other root vegetables. Very often, in the summer when the weather was hot, I would take a table out onto the staff room patio and they would do the veg out there in the sun. I frequently did it on my own if the girls were very busy or wanted to get away early.

The cleaning and kitchen girls didn't meet up very often as one shift finished lunchtime and the other didn't start until half past two. Vera was in contact with everyone as she was doing both jobs most days.

Diane had shown an aptitude for cooking so Kate had grabbed her more and more until she was almost off the cleaning rota altogether. However, she would fill in if someone was ill or on holiday.

Elaine came in to replace Diane and now we could cope with anything. Most days we needed three on the rota to get through the work if all the sixteen rooms were in use. Someone extra might then come into the kitchen to do the vegetables. Alternatively, whoever was in the potwash the night before would come in earlier to make a start on them.

Anyway, Elaine also had two boys so here were yet two more for the crèche. It took a lot of worry from all these mums knowing that they could bring the children.

Elaine's husband, Chris, was an excellent plumber and did a lot of work for us.

Soon after Elaine started, our water supply stopped, and Chris was called. He and John went up to the well. Everything seemed to be alright except that the filter had slipped out of place. There was plenty of water so back down they came. The blockage – or leak, was somewhere in the half mile of pipe. What a thought – this could be disasterous. Don't panic – take it a step at a time. One's thoughts tend to rush ahead. Cancel the dinner bookings and guests! Close the hotel and book them in somewhere else!

Chris started digging where the water entered the house. The alkathene pipe was one and a half inches and then had to reduce to the house pipe. When he undid the reducing joint he straight away found what was blocking everything – a frog! The poor thing must have been transported at great speed, head first, all the way underground until it met the narrower pipe. Needless to say, it didn't survive the experience!

We were immensely relieved to find the problem so easily as it could have taken forever.

John immediately replaced the old filter and had the water checked. There was now no possibility of anything else finding it's way into the well. Chris said that he had unblocked many pipes but this was the most interesting!

He and Elaine lived very close in Burry Green so it couldn't be more convenient. Elaine was fairly quiet and very nervous. A perfect target for Gill!

Marian or I would tell the girls when bedrooms were vacated so that they could get on with the cleaning. Gill told Elaine that 215 was ready for her to do so in she went. Unbeknown to her, Gill had made a 'body' in the bed that looked very realistic and Gill was hiding in the bathroom calling out sweet nothings to it. Poor Elaine, backed out spluttering apologies and shot downstairs to confess what she'd done. She did eventually see the funny side of it!

Another time, Gill smeared a lot of brown putty in the lavatory bowl and sent Elaine in first! She was a lot of fun. Elaine soon toughened up and got her own back.

Chapter Sixteen

My mother was beginning to get more and more forgetful. She was also repeating herself and I would hear the same story several times. She was finding it more difficult managing on her own and Jo arranged for a home help to come in a few times a week. They were very patient but the same cannot be said of her. They couldn't do anything right as far as she was concerned and they were replaced one after the other. There eventually was one that gave as good as she got and they rubbed along.

Her flat was on the first floor and had a second floor with three bedrooms and a bathroom so there were quite a lot of stairs. Jo and I decided to bring her bed down to the sitting room to make it easier as I was worried about her falling. She didn't want us to do this as she thought it would spoil the room but after we had finished she was quite pleased and agreed it was very comfortable. The room was sunny and near the kitchen. I had also bought a commode so she didn't have to worry about any stairs. She was falling quite a lot and I was really worried about what to do for the best. I bought her a 'help' telephone system and she always wore the button around her neck in case she had an accident. This wasn't much good as she kept ringing it by mistake or to chat with the volunteer on the other end of the phone. She didn't understand it at all.

I was going to see her most days. Jo did Sundays as on that day my feet didn't touch the ground! The home help would leave some lunch on the days she was in and Jo or I would take it every other day. She always looked forward to something sweet for tea and one of our desserts was always met with a smile.

My mother had always had such a sharp mind and knew what I was up to almost before I did. Such a very wise woman who had always been infallible to me in years gone by. A strong, forceful character who was now turning more into a wilful bully constantly making cruel comments. I was finding it hard to accept that this was happening to her. She had always had a horror of 'going off it' but now, thank God, she didn't realise it was happening to her.

Jo had recently got married. Bill was a wonderful man and took it on himself to visit my mother regularly. He was really caring and ignored her rudeness. She always called him 'Bob' for some reason. There had never been a Bob in the family so I don't know where that name came from. Anyway, Bill had a key and would pop in at various times which helped a lot.

I couldn't help going – I was having a tongue-lashing too but she was my mother and I loved her, come what may.

She was still fairly lucid – just forgetful with a lack of concentration. There were times that she couldn't work out the remote control for the television.

She somehow developed a bad chest infection and was admitted to hospital for a few days. I thought it would be a good idea to arrange for her to go into a local nursing home to see how it would work out. She liked people around her and she might enjoy it. I told her it was a convalescent home and if she didn't like it she didn't have to stay. I paid a week's fees and she had a nice room of her own.

I visited her the next day and was so upset to see her sitting amongst the others who were all asleep. The whole place was smelly and awful. The expression on her face said it all and I packed her few things and took her away.

I had always promised her that she would stay in her own home and I felt so guilty for trying to con her into this move.

We would carry on as we were.

We made a mistake in not digging the lake deeper. The reeds were spreading out and there was a weed covering the surface at great speed. We couldn't face getting the digger again and all that would entail.

John detailed three of the potwash boys for 'extra duty'. They went down to the lake with the rubber dinghy in their wet suits and waded in. The plan was to pull everything out by the roots and pile it on to the dinghy which was then pushed ashore. The weeds were transferred into the trailer which was then towed away on the back of the tractor, and dumped. They took it in turns to drive the tractor although they had a job to get Lynne's son, Gareth, off it. He took it upon himself to be foreman (just like his mother) and they had a whale of a time! I went down one afternoon to see how they were getting on and could hear wild Red Indian whoops as the three of them paddled the boat in and out of the islands. Best day's work they'd ever had!

John gave them the choice of getting on with the job, or enjoying the pleasure of it at a lower hourly rate. I think they took the latter.

I often thought back over the years when Fairyhill had been an elegant country mansion. Its various owners had entertained lavishly and it had been one of the coveted venues where people craved an invitation.

In those days it had taken twenty-three staff to run everything. It struck me that what we were doing was a modern version of the old days. Wasn't Fairyhill still a place where local people loved to visit? They were welcomed, dined and entertained. We still had about the same number of staff. The only difference was that now they paid for the pleasure!

I had drawn up a good plan for extending the Billiard room. It could be easily done without spoiling anything. We would lose the staff room patio but that was very rarely used.

We could build out over this which would more than double the size of the seating area and beneath it we would have another huge room with bar and cloakrooms. This would mean that wedding parties up to one hundred and fifty could enter through, and park in the big walled garden without approaching the main house at all. They would have their own private reception and bar and easy access to the grounds. We would make another two doors in the billiard room, one leading straight to the kitchen through the pantry and another to the private rooms below. This would mean we could take bigger weddings and they could remain throughout the evening in their private room, thus not disturbing anyone.

I thought we could esily have some sort of attractive partition dividing the billiard room so that it could revert to its smaller size for more intimate evenings.

Fairyhill just seemed to lend itself so readily to any ideas we had.

It was working with us, as though trying to pay back the help we had given.

Having worked this out down to its final detail on my 'squares', I was quite pleased. I hadn't told John about my idea and thought hard and long. We were receiving enquiries for weddings by the hundred every year and this would mean at least, two weddings a week. We'd make a fortune! But, wait a minute – is this what we wanted? It would mean separate staff to run them and almost a second kitchen staff on those days. We would also run the risk of spoiling the intimacy we had created. I decided to keep the idea to myself!

We were finding it hard to cope now. We had learnt from the shop days that you are only as good as your staff, and there is also a limit as to how far anyone can spread themselves. Let's keep to what is a winning formula and leave well alone.

We had paid off our loan to the WDA so were not as desperate to take every money making project put to us. We could afford to wind down a little.

During one of our 'exhausted' phases, we actually decided to try to sell Fairyhill and instructed Knight, Frank & Rutley. By the time the brochure was printed we were back to normal so were quite half hearted about any enquiries. Not that we had many. One group were interested but it transpired that they wanted to build 'chalets' in the grounds. Planning would have been against that even if we hadn't.

Things had changed so much since we first decided to buy. From the time when we only intended to renovate part of the house. It was easy then to put so much effort into the wood stripping, but gradually, we did more and more. If someone had told me at the start that I would handle and strip every single piece of wood in the whole of Fairyhill, I wouldn't have believed it possible. Sixty-six window sashes and frames, about sixty doors plus french doors, architraves, skirtings and shutters. The fact was that I moved on a bit at a time and it gradually 'happened'. That house had a personality of its own – it forced us on. At the start, I thought that there would have to be a ghost, so many people had lived and died there over the centuries. I did very often smell apple tart and custard at the top of the kitchen steps in the early renovating days, but nothing manifested itself. Maybe we had frightened it away with all the disturbance!

Our next plan had been the bed and breakfast through the summer. That would have been quite sensible, in retrospect, and we would have had the whole winter to recover. On the other hand, we wouldn't have met all the world famous celebrities that were entering our lives through the hotel. It was hard to believe that they were finding their way to this dot on the map. People were hearing about us all over the world now. Was that really Richard Dreyfuss throwing sticks for Celyn or Lord Jellicoe talking to Kate in the kitchen?

Although we were so busy, contrary to everything we had been warned against, we had only one thing stolen which upset me a lot . Everyone was welcome to read our books but I had a special one written by a friend of mine, Daniel Jones. He was the 'Dan' referred to in many of Dylan Thomas's stories and had written his own account of their childhood, 'My Friend Dylan Thomas'. Dan had written a personal message to me in this and someone had permanently 'borrowed' it. Nothing else had gone – our personal treasures were all through the house and were appreciated and enjoyed by everyone. Not even a towel had ever been missed. I hated the hotel hangers that are fixed to the wardrobe rails so we had nice wooden ones onto which I drew the word 'Fairyhill'. Maybe the occasional one would go missing but more often that not, by mistake, I'm sure. We have always thought the best of people and I think they respond accordingly.

We only had two bounced cheques in nine years, which must be a pretty good record. The first was from a family who stayed in the Coach House. Husband, wife and two small children. The man had come to Swansea for the power boat racing and had a huge expensive boat which had the luxury of its own engineer who also stayed in the Coach House. I didn't like the husband much – he was very brash – but the wife was sweet. I felt sorry for her and arranged for Emma to babysit whenever required. I also did all their washing free of charge as there is always such a lot with small children.

The two of them ate in the restaurant every night and had expensive wine. On two occasions they had Krug champagne at £72 per bottle. He said he only liked the best!

I suppose we should have seen it coming, but if you're not looking for it you don't see it. Their bill came to about £1,500 and we didn't get a penny. He had drawn the cheque on his firm's account knowing he was going bankrupt. The thought of him guzzling the best of everything, knowing that he couldn't pay was very galling.

The second experience was quite unbelievable and I would defy anyone not to be taken in.

An elderly white haired lady like 'Miss Marple' all alone, and we all fussed over her and worried about her being lonely. She had no transport so John drove her everywhere. She only had one 'sun suit' and one dress for the evening; I washed and ironed them every alternate day. On the days she didn't go to the beach, she would sit in the Stable garden and we would take her tea. She was a pillar of the chapel and we knew her whole life story. She thought Fairyhill and all the staff were wonderful and thanked everyone time and time again for looking after her. No one had ever been so kind to her and God would reward us all. Well, no one rewarded us – her cheque bounced and bounced and bounced. Obviously a seasoned performer!

Apart from these two instances, we fared very well compared to what we were told to expect.

Even our carpets were standing up well to the punishment they were receiving. We deliberately had patterns so that helped, of course. But they were such good quality and they seemed to respond to a light sponging if we had any bad stains. We had been told never to have good carpets industrially cleaned.

We were glad also that we had washable seat covers on our dining room chairs. It seems to me that all small children wipe their sticky hands on their seats! It didn't matter with ours – we could easily wash them clean and polish them up. Celyn liked Sunday lunchtimes after the children. She could go in later and 'hoover' under their tables!

Kate's food was getting better and better. We were listed in the top ten restaurants in Wales in the 'Good Food Guide' so we had high standards to maintain. There were a lot of food competitions that we were advised to enter but I never seemed to have the time to prepare all the applications and paper work and the restaurant was too busy to enable us to release Kate to enter them.

I've always thought there is more to a restaurant than good food.

The atmosphere has to be right too. We had both – a lovely 'feel' to the restaurant and Kate's excellent food.

She had all the help she needed now in the kitchen and Julie and Jay were doing more and more. There were Diane, Lis, Annette, Jane and also in addition, Melloney* who was Lis's sister-in-law and came in occasionally in addition to waitressing.

During school holidays, we also had two sisters, Sally and Katie who lived in Cilonnen. They started off waitressing but more and more Katie was finding herself in the kitchen.

They weren't there all the time, of course, but available to be called upon. Sometimes Kate would be too relaxed and would end up in a panic about half past six because she was nowhere near ready. Then the pressure would rise and the tensions spread through us all. If there was a lot of chat and laughter through the afternoon, I would say "Can we panic early today please, and chat later if there's time."

I often told Kate that the first diners would be in the bar at quarter past seven – fifteen minutes earlier than they actually were, so that I'd be sure to have them in the dining room without a delay. We never took them in until the starters were ready. Better to wait in the bar with company rather than on their own in the dining room. If we were late with the first table it was difficult to catch up.

We served complimentary crisp hot cockles to everyone as they arrived. I was very proud of this invention and everybody loved them – even those who didn't like cockles. We coated the wet cockles with flour and deep fried them. Crisp, with a sprinkling of salt – declicious. At one time John wanted to air-tight bag them like crisps to sell country wide, but he never had time. Perhaps in the future!

I remember one evening in the kitchen dinner was being served, and it was a hectic time. Kate was sending out an order and the finishing touch on one plate was a garnish comprising a sort of small pancake. It was all ready to go – the pancake had just been cooked and she was transfering it from the pan to the plate. She thought she had put it down somewhere and was frantically leaping around searching. She got everyone in a tizz. Vera was standing patiently, holding

---

* This is how Melloney spells her name.

the plate, waiting for the missing garnish. It was Lynne who eventually spotted it. She was laughing so much, all she could do was point. There it was – stuck fast to the top of Kate's foot! Vera very quickly left with the order – minus the garnish! What a hoot!

Needless to say, the kitchen was on stop until everyone had recovered themselves.

As we had no mains supply of gas, we relied on the Liquid Bulk gas tanker topping us up every three weeks or so. We had a vast storage tank and it was a very satisfactory arrangement until we had a new driver and he missed us out! I noticed the drop in pressure slightly as I was cooking breakfasts and, yes, it would be a Sunday morning. We were full for lunch as usual, and by the time the girls arrived at nine o'clock John was practically frothing at the mouth. He had, of course, already telephoned the gas company and they would be coming. The tanker was somewhere in Somerset but it had been contacted and would be with us as soon as possible.

Our girls were wonderful and thought it all out. The lamb was taken down to Lynne in Llangennith to go into her oven and the beef was to go over to Rhossili with Diane. The sirloin would have to be cut in three but then it would go into her oven. Diane and Melloney went with the beef and also all the vegetables. Jay stayed to make the desserts and starters and we telephoned for Jane to come in to help. We had to deep fry the roast potatoes and hoped we would have the gas in time for the Yorkshire puddings. We would be alright for the cockles as they were also done in the electric fryer.

It was so tense – John was pacing up and down and kept going outside to see if he could hear the tanker. Eventually, he ran to the kitchen door, "Listen, listen, there's something big coming!" This was about midday and all was well. We made it – thanks to such a willing group of sensible women!

The only other time a similar thing happened was when an electricity transformer had been damaged in a storm. Our supply had gone off quite early in the morning and the Electricity Board couldn't give us any indication of how long we would be without. They had to locate the position of the transformer first! Again, as luck would have it, we had a dinner party booked for that evening – Morganite with thirty-two guests. A set meal that had been planned for weeks. The time was passing and still no electricity. Although we cook by gas, it was winter and our kitchen was very dark, impossible to cook without light. We MUST get a generator.

The Electricity Board still couldn't give us any hope and by four o'clock we had to make a decision. We could hold on and hope but we had to think of our guests. They had to make alternative arrangements. We had to cancel. John telephoned and told them the bad news. He had already telephoned Colin Pressdee in Drangway, and yes, Colin would take them! We lost a lot of money but more importantly, we felt we had let down one of our favourite clients. The electricity came on at about half past seven – in time for our residents but everyone else we had cancelled. All the Electricity Board could say was, more or less, 'hard luck'. Definitely no apology whatsoever.

Chapter Seventeen

Marian had received a telephone call from Decca Recording Company asking if we would be prepared to take a block booking at any time. She told them that we would be delighted and they said they would get back to us. We heard nothing more and assumed that was the end of the matter.

Their Personnel Officer eventually contacted us, saying that she had already made one visit to our hotel and would be coming again for Sunday lunch with a few more people to have a look around. She said the intended booking might entail some world famous singers staying and what would our reaction be if we were asked to produce something to eat in the middle of the night. I though this a strange question and apparently said (I was told years after that my answer was what swayed them) that I was sure I could come up with something easily enough!

She duly came for lunch with Brian McMasters, the Musical Director and Leader of the Welsh National Opera orchestra and they all enjoyed their lunch before having a good look around, inside and out.

It transpired that they would be doing a recording of the opera 'Adriana Lecouvrer' with Joan Sutherland and Luciano Pavarotti as the principals. Dame Joan's husband, Richard Bonynge would be conducting.

They wanted a country venue within a thirty-five mile radius of Cardiff which is the home of the Welsh National Opera. This was so that the orchestra could come to the singers rather than the expense of everyone going to London. Sian, the Personnel Officer had been searching for the right hotel from Chepstow down and liked Fairyhill and its atmosphere so much that they were prepared to travel the extra distance. We were really flattered and, of course, so excited. Sian looked at all the rooms and decided who was going where. They would be here for ten days in September and another ten days in

December. Pavarotti had only one day's recording in September so he wouldn't stay then but would be here in December. She thought the Bonynges would have room 211 and Pavarotti would be in the Coach House or Stable where he would have his own kitchen.

The time passed slowly while we waited for this unbelievable happening. I was only sorry that my mother couldn't share in my excitement. I told her, of course, Joan Sutherland had always been her favourite but she really couldn't grasp what I was telling her.

I had a phone call from a lady who had stayed at Fairyhill a few times over the years. She had something to do with the Pavarotti Fan Club in this country and had heard that he would be staying with us. She wanted to know all the details. I told her the dates had not been confirmed but she was most persistent. I eventually managed to fend her off. I had visions of hundreds of fans converging on us!

The four engineers arrived first, about three days before the musicians. The recording was taking place in the Brangwyn Hall in Swansea and they had to set up all the microphones and miles of wires, an extremely skilled job which had to be absolute perfect by the time the others came.

Bryn Terfel was the first of the artistes to arrive under his own steam. This was 1988 and he was still virtually unknown. A large young man with an easy-going manner and very unspoilt. We soon felt as though we had known him forever and the first thing he did was take Celyn for a walk. He said she was just like his dog.

Bryn was more excited than we were. It was his first major recording and he couldn't believe that he was part of the same cast as these mega stars. After the first day's recording he showed me his score with everyone's signatures.

Next came Joan Sutherland driven in the Decca limo with a companion and Sian. I was almost too overwhelmed to function. Sian introduced us and I took her up to her room. I needn't have worried, she was so down to earth and easy and she was thanking me! I said I didn't know what to call her, Mrs. Bonynge or Dame Joan. She said, "My dear Midge, whatever you like, I answer to anything."

She had come from her home in Switzerland but her husband was travelling independently as he was coming direct from a concert in

New York. He was a tall elegant man, very good looking and charming. He had a lot of luggage and, as usual, John began carrying it upstairs. I caught his bulging eyes as he tried to lift two of the cases. He was too little and they were too heavy. Apparently, they were full of scores! Bryn was standing in the hall chatting and leapt to John's help. He was so huge and picked up both cases as though they were hat boxes! John asked him to stand by for the departures!

The others arrived throughout the next two days. Leo Nucci, a gorgeous Italian baritone who also loved Celyn instantly. He had two dogs of his own and a country house so he appreciated the surroundings. He walked around the grounds muttering "Bella, bella". He was a real charmer and all the girls fought to serve him!

Francesco Ellera D'Artagne, a bass, who spoke a little more English than Leo Nucci, was equally easy to please.

Cleopatra Ciurca flew in from Sydney and we didn't see her for two days – she slept most of the time. She was jet lagged and had deliberately arrived two days before her part was due to be recorded so that she had time to recover.

Michel Senechal was a tenor who was also the Musical Director of the Paris Opera house.

The rest of the party consisted of Sian's assistant Jane, and Andrew Cornall, the Producer. There were various other bodies who came and went throughout the recording but they were staying at the then Holiday Inn.

The procedure was that the recording sessions were held from midday until six o'clock and throughout the mornings, voice coachings and individual rehearsals would take place in our drawing room! How unbelievable! I saw that this door was always left slightly open and it was surprising how often my work took me past that room!

Pavarotti's session was on the third day and it was agreed that we could attend. We could only spare an hour but this was a chance in a lifetime. Always seeing the great man in front of a vast audience, it was a thrilling experience to be sitting in this empty hall. There was the orchestra, Richard Bonynge, John and me and the big man himself, standing there in a shirt and blue jeans. To think that he would be staying with us in three months time. We just hoped that we could live up to his requirements.

That evening, the engineers and Producer were sitting in the bar talking very earnestly. Of course, one never listens deliberately (well, hardly ever) but I couldn't help hearing the gist of what the conversation was about. That day's recording hadn't gone very well and Mr. P. was to be replaced. I couldn't help myself, "Does this mean he won't be staying with us?" That was the least of their worries, I'm sure. It was such a disappointment but, never mind, we had lots of other wonderful people.

They were a super group who all got on so well. Everyone was on first name terms from the Producer to the lorry driver. They were a team and if they were all back together, they would eat at the same table. We were permanently on our toes, ready to push tables together or split them again.

Sian had somehow discovered that it was Cleopatra's birthday. She told me and I arranged with Kate for her to make a surprise of some sort. Everyone was seated around a large table when Cleopatra walked in still a little bleary eyed. I came behind her carrying a little meringue swan with a lighted candle and everyone started singing. She was quite overwhelmed – and so were we. Never was there such a powerful rendering of 'Happy Birthday'. What voices! If the wine glasses hadn't been full they would undoubtedly have shattered!

Throughout the stay an assortment of colourful characters would appear from different parts of the world to talk over various productions or plans. One gentleman was Dame Joan's costume 'builder'. He had come from London with a dress to give her a fitting and they closeted themselves in the Conference Room. Some of the costumes are so enormous and heavy that they stand up on their own. She is a large lady and this one weighed a ton. It was all so exciting – for the time they were with us, I felt I was living in a different world.

The weather was warm and sunny and they were seeing everything at its best. John made sure he took them, two or three at a time, to see our wonderful coast. They went to Rhossili and walked around to Fall Bay and to Oxwich beach along to Tor. The Italians couldn't believe the scenery and the expanses of sand, and kept asking where all the people were! Why weren't the beaches crowded? We were pleased to show off our little piece of Wales and I know they went home with a different outlook. It was such a change from their usual major city hotel scene.

I would have loved to spend hours at the recording sessions. I

Midge, Kate, Dame Joan and John

found it fascinating. The Conductor was linked to the Producer in the control room by telephone and either could stop the other whenever necessary. A portion would be recorded then the artiste and Conductor go to the control room and it would be played back. The sound coming through the vast speakers was amazing. As it was played back, any imperfection was marked and would then be re-recorded. I always went into the control room – I could see the stage on a TV set and hear all that was said between Producer and Conductor. I kept very quiet and tried not to be noticed.

The only artiste who didn't come in to listen to her piece was Joan Sutherland. She left that to her husband and stayed sitting on the stage doing her tapestry.

Of course, there was a tremendous amount of extra laundry with this many people staying for a long period. I didn't mind – it's not that I enjoy doing it normally but I always think it's such an intimate thing to do and I felt almost privileged. I was actually ironing Leo Nucci's shirts and folding Joan Sutherland's underwear. I even enjoyed starching and ironing a frilly dress shirt of Richard Bonynge's!

The Bonynges had asked for breakfast in bed every day. Just toast and coffee for Dame Joan and a basket of fresh fruit for her husband. Would it be possible to have it at eight o'clock? Actually, when they were leaving, they remarked that this was the only place they had had their breakfast on time. In large hotels it was always half an hour late or half an hour early. We were small enough to care. She never saw John and me standing outside the bedroom door giggling. John looking at the big hand on his watch with fist poised ready to knock! Nothing was by chance.

She was such an unassuming lady and would often sit out in the garden with her needlework. "Sit and talk to me, Midge." She signed autographs for all the girls and asked about their children and was so easy.

She asked me one day to arrange a hair appointment. Well, I cut my own hair so don't know anything about hairdressers. I said the nearest, as far as I knew, was in Swansea but she didn't want to go that far. Any little one locally would do. John telephoned a tiny hairdresser in Scurlage and made an appointment. It was a very humble place with lino on the floor and I'm sure she'd never seen anything like it. John took her and picked her up and she said everything was fine. John did tell them who to expect but I don't think they knew who she was. Anyway, she went there again and also on her subsequent visits, so she must have been pleased.

Whether or not to allow smoking was a constant headache. It's not easy to determine beforehand whether the members of a party are smokers or non-smokers. It didn't matter so much in the bar or drawing room as people had the freedom to move around but the dining room was a different matter. I wrote on the top of the menus 'If you cannot refrain from smoking please do so with consideration for other diners' This seemed to do the trick and people would wait until their meal was over and then have coffee and cigarettes in the drawing room or bar. Some desperate souls would pop out between extended course intervals. Most were very considerate. If there were only a few people in the dining room I would check all the tables to ask if anyone objected, then I could give the go ahead.

I remember one particular night when we were very full, and a couple arrived who hadn't booked. There was one table for two left in the dining room so they were lucky. Everyone else was well on with their meals by the time they went in for their starters. I remember that they had a very nice bottle of wine and foie gras to begin.

Very soon Vera came to me to say that they had asked for an ash tray. I hated this but knew I had to go to see them. They had already 'lit up'. To make matters even worse, on the next table were six of our Decca party, three of whom were singers.

I approached the couple, smiling and apologetic and very politely asked if they would mind waiting until after their main course before smoking. They immediately put the cigarettes out and I thought that was the end of it. I left gratefully, very relieved.

Almost immediately, Vera found me again to say that they wanted to see the Manager. I thought, 'Whooops, here we go' I took a deep breath and went in again. They were furious and asked for the bill. I apologised again and hoped that they would understand that I had to consider the majority and if they only waited a short while, everyone else would have finished eating and would leave them in peace. They were most abusive and uncouth. I was quite relieved when they said they would tell all their friends not to come to Fairyhill. I told them there would be no bill and was quite proud of myself that I kept my dignity throughout a most unpleasant and upsetting experience.

It was some consolation that I had a formal letter of thanks from Decca a few weeks later!

Only one other 'smoking' incident occurred. It was in the Billiard room this time and concerned a family of four who had booked in for three nights. The father had asked for an ashtray so, of course, I had been told. (John never seemed to be around on these occasions!) As I approached the table I could see that he had quite a sizeable cigar in his hand, as yet unlit. He was the only one that had finished his main course, the others were still eating. The billiard room was busy and I was even more on edge as I knew some people there were violently anti-smoking! I really, really hated this part of my job. I just had to stop him lighting it.

I pointed out politely that most people were just starting their main courses and if he could possibly wait for them to finish eating I was sure they would appreciate it. He didn't say anything but the cigar was put away and I thanked him.

We were busy and I hadn't seen John to tell him what had happened so he was very taken aback later, when this same man pounced on him in the hall telling John to cancel his next two nights as he wasn't staying any longer than he had to. I think John probably blamed me for losing the booking but I did what I thought I had to. Personally, I'd let everyone do what they liked. Smoking doesn't bother me. We probably breath in worse things than tobacco smoke. It's just not possible to please everyone and I was upset. Praised by the non-smokers and condemned by the smokers!

We had many coincidences – a couple from a small English village staying with us, meeting people from the same village. We even had a Swiss family who met friends at Fairyhill, neither knowing the others would be there. We hoped they were all with their right spouses!

The most amazing coincidence was when one of our regular diners, who happened to be the Principal of the University, was entertaining Lord Sharpe and his wife for dinner. They were having a pre dinner drink in the bar, when Lord Sharpe noticed a signed photograph of Vladimir Ashkenazy, the Russian pianist and conductor hanging on our wall. He was most interested and told us that they had almost met a few years back. I could hardly get my words out – "Well, Lord Sharpe, you may have your chance tonight, he happens to be staying here again. He'll be back from his recording any minute and we can introduce you."

As they were walking into the hall to go into the dining room the front door opened and Ashkenazy came in with Andrei Gavrilov, his recording partner. He is such a warm, friendly man and I knew he wouldn't mind the introduction.

Professor Clarkson couldn't wait to tell me the story and called me to their table almost as soon as they were seated. Apparently, having defected from Russia years ago, Ashkenazy had eventually returned to Moscow after twenty-five years. This was the first time he had seen his parents in all that time and a huge concert had been organised in Moscow where he was to conduct. I did remember seeing this on television. Well, the coincidence was that it had been Lord Sharpe who had sponsored the whole concert and had, in fact, been sitting next to Ashkenazy's father! Something had cropped up which prevented them meeting then.

Well, could you believe it? From Moscow to Fairyhill. I thought it was a wonderful story and to see them both chatting away in our hall was a great thrill.

Fairyhill had two sets of gates and opposite the ones between the Stable and the Coach House, across the other side of the lane was the original farmyard. The stone built barns had half fallen down but a local farmer, Mathias Taylor from Llangennith had been paying a nominal rent for years and used some for storage. There were three fields comprising fifteen acres which stretched down to the main road at Stembridge and he used these for grazing.

The previous owners of Fairyhill had been trying for years to regain possession of the farm from Mathias and I believe court proceedings had even taken place, all to no avail. Both parties, like two immovable objects and very antagonistic towards each other – a real feud! It even came to water pipes being cut through!

We knew Mathias was a strange man from other episodes we had heard and also our own experience. He had told us years later that he knew what happened to our lovely lost dog, Caleb. We had visualised Caleb suffering terribly, but no amount of pleading would persuade Mathias to tell what he knew – if anything. It was just his way.

We had decided to restore and convert these farmbuildings so needed to get vacant possession. We thought a different approach was called for regarding the farmyard. We told Mathias that if he vacated the buildings, we would sell him the two lower fields at a sensible price. He was his usual non commital self at the offer but we knew he was delighted so the situation resolved itself very amicably.

We retained the five-acre-field adjacent to the farmyard. It was quite hilly and from the top one could see down Stembridge Valley in the North then up to Burry Green. Southwards was Hill End Farm where Tom lived and Cefn Bryn to our well. It was a beautiful spot with lovely trees. Across the east boundary of Banky Field, as it was apparently called, was a public footpath with a stile each end. We must try to remember to keep these open and bramble free.

We were going to make a start on the first Barn. I drew up the plans in the same way but gave them to a different architect this time. I didn't want to offend him but after the last experience I felt I had to make things clear that this was the design I wanted. I didn't need any show of initiative. Of course, if something wasn't possible, and if levels didn't tie up, I would understand. As long as it was all explained to me and made sense.

The Barn was to be similar to the Stable in as much as the main room would be enormous and open up to the rafters. There would be a large en suite bedroom on the ground floor at one end approached under a deep two yard wide gallery, through an arched 'tunnel'. Above this would be a second en suite bedroom with a sloping ceiling. This led off the gallery. The stairs wound up and around inside the arched wooden entrance of the gallery. I could see it all. There would be a large kitchen/dining room leading off the sitting room again through an archway.

While doing this plan we decided that we would try to get Outline Planning passed for the other barns at the same time. We didn't anticipate any difficulty, but you never can tell. As it happens, it was refused, the reason being that ruined barns were thought to be of historic interest and should be left. Well, if these were left another ten years there would be a very uninteresting pile of stones! We wrote a few letters and with the help of our local councillor, it was passed on the second application. Good, now we could go!

Chapter Eighteen

The second phase of the Decca recording had started. The Bonynges were back with Carlo Bergonzi, a very famous tenor, now getting on in years, who had replaced Pavarotti.

Carlo Bergonzi was accompanied by his wife – a very powerful lady who escorted him everywhere making all the decisions and shielding him from everything. She seemed more the celebrity that he did and appeared in expensive flowing garments and thick furs. She never appeared for breakfast but had it in her room. He would come down on his own. His English was practically non-existent but we managed to make ourselves understood. He talked non stop in Italian to Celyn – she seemed to understand!

I was still managing the occasional trip into the recording sessions, but it was difficult. Between the hotel and visits to my mother, I couldn't be there too long. I loved listening to all the chat when they returned 'home' in the evenings. By this time, we knew them all quite well and were treated more like friends. They enjoyed the relaxed atmosphere and particularly, the food. Two of the engineers were quite young and had enormous appetites. One would often have an additional starter. The puddings would be gone through systematically and one night I remember, one of them ate seven crèmes brulées!

An evening that sticks in my mind, again concerns Professor Clarkson. He and his wife had come to eat with us and were discussing with some people in the bar the coincidence that had happened with Ashkenazy on their last visit. He jokingly asked who we had for him tonight. John reeled off a few names from the opera world and his jaw visibly dropped!

When he eventually managed to speak, he told us that they had seen Dame Joan at the Sydney Opera House the year before and they were two of her biggest fans. They were sitting at the next table to her in the Billiard Room and spent the evening, they said, trying not to stare!

John had the opportunity of introducing them to her later on. We knew she wouldn't mind and it positively made their year. They chatted for quite a while.

As they were leaving John said, "We can't keep this standard up, you know. Don't expect too much next time!"

On their last evening, the Decca Group wanted one large table so they could have a party. Other singers who were staying at the Holiday Inn; Thomas Hampson, Alison Hagley, Willard White and Daniel Washington, were invited together with the Director of the Welsh National Opera and the leader of the orchestra. About twenty-four in all. Kate put on a super meal and even invented a special pudding for Dame Joan.

It was now that she chose to announce that she had decided to retire. This was to be her last recording. Well, nearly everyone got up to say a few words about 'La Stupenda' and it was all very emotional.

It was sad to see them go. Dame Joan gave me a bunch of flowers and a big hug. She said how much they had enjoyed themselves and I know she meant it. In fact, we had a Christmas card from them re-

Original farmyard

Same view after completion

peating the fact! The engineers and producer we were to see many times more.

We decided to take a holiday. Another Christmas was over and we were leaving January 1st 1989. New Year's Eve was hectic and very busy but we had something to look forward to. We had chartered a yacht in the Caribbean with our friends, Bob and Ann.

They had spent the evening and night with us at Fairyhill and we all left for the airport at seven o'clock in the morning having had very little sleep.

So that we could go without worrying, we were closing for the whole of January. Marian would move in to look after Celyn, Winni and Annwyl, to man the telephone and see to anything that cropped up. A full staff would have to come in on January 2nd to clear up from New Year's Eve and to see to all the bedrooms and laundry. Marian would also have the lovely job of taking down the Christmas decorations.

We had a super holiday with Bob and Ann with lots of sunshine and we returned totally refreshed and ready for action. Nothing untoward had happened. Marian had enjoyed herself and had also taken lots of bookings. She had even accepted a few guests while we were away. Some of our regulars who were happy just to have bed and breakfast and go to the pub for an evening meal. She cooked the breakfasts – good old Marian!

Derek, our builder was back again to get started across the road. The first thing to do was knock down the wall and gate along the side of the road. I envisaged a wide open courtyard as the entrance to the farmyard and then a huge wall across from the Barn to the building opposite with an arched entrance through which to drive. I wanted to look from the road up through the archway. This sounded expensive and may be it wouldn't be feasible. Anyway, it was in my mind.

This area was cleared first and drains dug. A septic tank also had to be excavated at the bottom end of the field and trenches for gas and water pipes. We had already branched off our water pipe when originally laying it in case we should ever do anything with the farm.

Once this was done we could make a start on the Barn. This had been used for cattle and had feed troughs and old black floor tiles similar to those that had been in the Stable. We were to re-use these in various places.

When the basic work outside had been finished, Derek got started on the inside and thought it would take about four months. Most of the stonework was alright. It had to be underpinned and a large buttress built against the front wall to support it. This looked very attractive but was also essential! The original doorway was four feet wide, eight feet high and arched. We would need an extremely large door. Huge hinges and studded, I thought.

The builders were now into our way of doing things and there weren't so many 'Can't do thats'. We would install yet another woodstove. They were so wonderful and this would be our fourth of the same type. The Jotul No. 6, Norwegian and unbeatable in looks and performance. We had put one in Burry Cottage hall and Fairyhill hall and a third in the Stable. They needed a lot of dry wood but we had plenty. We discovered to our horror that the No. 6 was no longer stocked by anyone. In fact, it was thought to be no longer made. We advertised in the *Western Mail* and thankfully, had a reply from someone in Abergavenny.

We had the other half of our holly tree ready for the mantle above, so that was organised.

Derek always made sure that his men left the site tidied and swept every night. It was easy for me to go in with my plan and measuring tape to check on positions of doorways and walls. I would mark them out with pieces of wood along the ground and chalk on the walls. They would know better than to pick up a 'wall' before I had talked to them. Not very professional, but it worked.

I had marked the position of the woodstove and chimney so that I had room for a long narrow window to one side of it. I must have been too long between visits, as when next I went, the chimney had been hacked out in the wrong place – in the middle of the wall. Derek couldn't believe that anyone could want a stove off-centre, so I lost my window. I couldn't bring myself to make them fill in the wall again and hack out the chimney two feet further over. In retrospect, I wish I had – I've always regretted not having that little window to let in the morning sun.

Everything else went smoothly. The kitchen was so big that we decided to put a wall and door six feet from the pine end wall so that we had quite a large utility room to house the boiler, washing machine, dryer and fridge/freezer with plenty more storage space.

There was a stable door leading out onto a big patio that got all the morning and afternoon sun. This patio could also be reached through a door from the sitting room.

We managed to find time to furnish it, which took a bit of doing. We had a comfortable leather armchair and two big sofas in blue which went well with the carpet. We had learnt that leather stood up well over the years to quite hard wear. We found a lovely oak dresser in Ross on Wye and various other antiques. I wanted a very big tapestry for the wall but failed to find one. They say that necessity is the mother of invention and I had the brilliant idea of taking one of the old Persian rugs from the conservatory and hanging that on the wall. I made loops at the top and threaded a pole through – it looked magnificent and very dramatic.

We had king size zip and link beds again that could split to singles if necessary. We had these in the hotel. It meant we had to have both king-size and single duvets and covers. I bought enough matching covers and pillowcases for the cottages we hadn't yet done in case the pattern should be discontinued.

All we had to do now was connect telephones to the bedrooms

and we had yet two more letting rooms – 250 and 251. This would bring us up to eighteen rooms.

One of the first guests in the Barn was an ex prime Minister of Sri Lanka with a name none of us could pronounce.

At that time also we had a small wedding lunch booked consisting of only fourteen people. When they arrived, the bride's mother told me that they would be one less which meant thirteen around the table – very unlucky!

I told one of the girls to pop over to the Stable where my very large teddy bear lived. His name was Uska Dara. When I told Jay and Julie that Uska Dara would be sitting in the empty place they looked quite non plussed. "Will they mind?" says Julie. "I hope not, but it's only to make up the numbers," I replied.

They still looked unsure, but eventually realised I meant Uska Dara from the Stable and not the Sri Lankan from the Barn!

Our sign at the end of the lane at Stembridge had been vandalised several times over the years. It would be physically pulled off its supports and sometimes removed but more often than not, thrown over the wall. We were upset to think anyone would want to do this, but

Barn

190

Same view

on thinking it over, decided it must be late night revellers from Swansea returning from the King's Head in Llangennith. We had several new signs made over the years and apart from the expense, it was the inconvenience of being without it. We needed as many signs as possible for people to find us, we were so hidden away.

We had applied for permission to put up a sign on Llandewi Cross so that anyone travelling on the South Gower road would realise there was an hotel close by. We were refused this as it would be detrimental to the area.

We decided to bite the bullet and had a new sign painted which John and Terry took down and fixed to the road signpost. Almost immediately, we had 'people off the road' as we called those who arrived without previously booking. They all remarked that they would never have chanced upon us without the sign and we did really well for three days. After that, our sign was removed. We presumed by someone from the Council. We weren't doing very well with our signs!

We eventually solved the mystery of our vandalised sign. Terry was passing it one evening and actually saw a local farmer with a crow bar – caught in the act! How awful. And hurtful, to think that someone we know could be so vindictive. John was so incensed that he sent

Inside Barn

Sign at Llandewi

Roger, our local policeman, to warn the offender off, and after that our sign remained untouched.

If only I could delegate more, my life would be a lot easier. Why was I doing so much? It was as though I couldn't trust anyone to do things as well as I did. What conceit. Maybe it was something to do with my birth sign – Aries. But I didn't know much about that sort of thing. I would have to ask Guinevere. I did try occasionally, but I found it impossible to ignore even tiny details. That lace cloth was inside out. I could see the hem from here. Who did that? I might as well have done it myself in the first place, as I usually did. Now I would have to strip the table, turn the cloth and relay. Why not find the culprit and get them to rectify it? No. I'm cross. I'll do it myself and then I won't get more upset.

Perhaps, very rarely, John and I would go out for a meal. Always back by ten o'clock to see everyone for a chat. Into the dining room to find that the fire had gone out. Is there anything more depressing? Why on earth didn't somebody put coal on it?

I was forever checking the smallest details and trying to see things through the eye of a person sitting alone at a table 'nit picking'.

Why couldn't I get one of the girls to do the flowers? That took me ages. There was always a large arrangement in the inner hall, in one of the alcoves and then every table had its individual little vase. It seemed that no sooner had I spent all this time on them than they died! Everything recurred. Why wouldn't I be satisfied with someone else's way of doing things – it wouldn't be wrong, just different. My imagination was too vivid and I could see everything as pictures in my head. It was a quirk and I wasn't likely to change now, so I'd have to make the best of things. I was doing a lot – breakfasts, laundry, flowers, dining rooms, menus, weddings, wine, gardening, seeing my mother, watching the builders and that was all before starting 'work'! At least the kitchen ran without me interfering.

John saw to the grounds, all shopping, promotions, the thousand and one things that crop up on the administration side, banking, and of course, the bar. We were a good team and were standing up to the strain pretty well. It was only the fact that we got on so well that our marriage was surviving this. Bed was for collapsing into – too tired for any more activity! No one who hasn't experienced extreme fatigue can appreciate the exquisite pleasure of lying horizontal on a comfy bed with all the weight taken off throbbing legs. I have even forced myself to stay awake so I can extend the sheer pleasure of 'stopping'.

Although we were working so hard physically, we were very healthy. Never ever ill. We used to joke about it and say we never had time. No flu bug could catch us – we moved too fast. I think it was mostly determination and adrenalin that kept me going. I was always looking ahead to the next job and anticipating every incident that might occur.

It was very gratifying to run an establishment in exactly the way we wanted without having to account to anyone. John had run the shop in this way but always in the background was his brother.

We knew that everyone enjoyed working for us and it showed in their attitude. This didn't apply so much to the kitchen staff, although I'm pretty sure they also enjoyed themselves, but cleaners and waitresses had a lot of freedom and I know, felt part of a family with John and me at the head.

Our guests appreciated the staff – both cleaners and waitresses, and there was a polite but easy atmosphere between them.

Relaxed diners lend themselves to an extra treat. Vicky always thought of it as a challenge to sell everyone a glass of dessert wine with their puds and we would go through bottles when she was on duty!

John, Midge, Jay, Kate, Jenny and Julie

Lynne specialised in Vintage Port and had the same attitude. They never laboured the point but would make the suggestion whilst chatting and not many refused.

We also sold quite a lot of our own Sloe Gin. We had always made it every year and had quite a stock. It was kept for at least five years and was delicious!

Although we hadn't had much of a response when we had advertised the sale of Fairyhill, it was now 1989 and it was in our minds to sell. We were discussing this with Kate and one thing led to another. She would give anything to buy it. How wonderful! Her boyfriend Clive, was an accountant so he disappeared with our books for the weekend and we all got very excited.

We would sell the Coach House with the hotel and live in the Stable. Well, as very often happens after the first flush of excitement, reality creeps in and unfortunately, this never happened. Much as she wanted it and much as we could do certain things to help, it wasn't possible. It was nice while it lasted but now, let's put it all behind us and get on with the job.

Towards the end of that year Kate had gone to France on holiday, as she always did. After a week she telephoned us to say she wasn't coming back. She had decided to take a job managing an hotel in Chamonix. She was fed up with cooking and wanted a change. I suppose the idea of buying Fairyhill had unsettled her and turned her mind onto a different course. She had been with us for five years and it was quite a shock, to go like that without warning. Now we were in a pickle.

We had big discussions with Julie and Jay and we decided that they would be more than capable of carrying on without employing a more senior chef. They had worked closely with Kate for two and a half years and they were very confident that they could cope. Julie had been with us a few months longer so was technically senior, but we felt they were equally capable and gave them the same pay and accolades.

I wouldn't have believed that things could have gone so well. There was quite a relaxed feel in the kitchen and they were always ready by seven o'clock.

The food was still good although we were automatically dropped from the 'Good Food Guide' as our chef had left. We nevertheless continued to have heaps of compliments even though we had lost Kate. We were so relieved!

There was still a lot of laughter in the kitchen. I remember one evening when they wanted to get their own back on one of our regulars who was always coming in to the kitchen to tease them. We had rabbit on the menu and he was the only one on his table who had ordered it. On the back window of Julie's car was stuck a 'Roger Rabbit' doll. She shot out through the back door and came back with this. When it was time for the main course to go to that table, Lynne went into the restaurant, plate in each hand. "Who ordered the beef, please? Thank you. And the rabbit?" Pause … down went the plate of Roger Rabbit in front of the man who was the 'victim' and the whole table exploded! He took it all in good part and appreciated the joke more than anyone!

Another of our gentlemen came as often as he could. He was a barrister and always made sure he stayed at least one night. He really enjoyed his food and would study the menu as soon as he arrived. He was usually down to eat early and liked to stretch his meal out so that it lasted the evening. As much as anything he enjoyed the breakfasts, especially our poached eggs. He wanted to know how I did them so that he could tell his wife (I didn't think that would go down very well). On his next trip he said they hadn't been able to do them properly so he came into the kitchen while I showed him. Saucepan of simmering water, a little white wine vinegar, then drop them in – easy. Watch them carefully. He tried a few on his own until he was happy. He brought his wife with him one Easter weekend and, during a conversation in the bar, he told a group of guests that Fairyhill did the best poached eggs he'd ever tasted. He had a 'carrying' voice and we were busy! The next morning I had orders for twenty-seven poached eggs! I thanked him for the compliment but asked if he could keep these announcements a little quieter. Poached eggs take care and attention, and it doubled the cooking time of breakfasts!

We had another breakfast compliment which pleased us immensely, but had nothing whatsoever to do with my cooking. Ashkenazy stood up one morning and said, "This is the best toast in the world!" Nancy Morgan's bread and John's speed serving it hot get the credit for that!

Chapter Nineteen

My mother was slipping more and more into her forgetful world. She kept telling me she was lonely and wanted to go home! What could one do if she was already home? It was getting to the stage when I wasn't happy leaving her on her own. She was incontinent and I felt her sheets should be changed more often. She got up only when I was there and then after an argument. It was terrible to see her like this and I had to do something. She loved her flat but now she didn't know she was in it. I spoke to Jo and made the decision to bring her down to me at Fairyhill. I put a bed downstairs in the lovely garden room of the Stable which looked out into the walled garden. She could sit out there when the weather was good.

I persuaded her easily but I don't think she really knew what was happening. We brought some of her furniture to make her feel at home and settled her in. Now I could spend more time with her without the thirty mile round trip to Mumbles every day. The girls could take it in turns to visit her when they had time. If only for five minutes, that would be enough to distract her.

It was quite a demanding schedule but I was happier to have her close. I went over at seven o'clock in the morning with a cup of tea. She was usually awake and I would draw the curtains back, change her bed and tidy up while she drank her tea. Then I gave her a wash and saw to her general toiletries before going back over to the kitchen to cook breakfasts. She was happy as long as she had the television or radio on.

When I had finished the guests' breakfasts I would take hers over and stay for a while. She still wanted to go 'home' but when I asked if she wanted to go back to the flat, she couldn't remember it. I think 'home' was somewhere in her childhood. It was terrible – my mother was gone, and I was heartbroken. All I could do now was to look after this old lady.

I registered her with our local doctors but she didn't need any

Mum and Midge in Stable

treatment. They suggested a District Nurse to help me, who would come three mornings a week to wash her. I thought this was wonderful. It didn't sound like the National Health Service that everyone was complaining about. The nurse was super and gave me a lot of moral support, but she naturally couldn't get to me early every time. I never knew when to expect her and spent too much time popping back and forth to the Stable to see if she had been. A couple of times it was afternoon when she got there by which time, of course, I had done all the necessaries. I thought her services would be needed more by people who couldn't cope. I could cope, so I continued my morning routine. This was impossible on busy Sundays and Bill and Jo would spend Saturday night so that Jo could be with my mother to give her breakfast and wash her. The earliest I could get over there would be about half past ten. I would usually find Jo still struggling to wash her with my mother fighting every inch.

All in all, we managed very well. She was in a beautiful room with me popping in throughout the day. Annwyl had found her way into the walled garden and through the cat flap so was more often than not to be found curled up on my mother's bed – they both loved it! I would take her a lovely lunch and tea then a sherry or gin and tonic before her dinner, and a Baileys or Tia Maria later on as a night cap. Top class hotel service!

John arranged to hire a wheelchair so that we could push her round to the front lawn for a change. Sometimes one of the girls would take her for a little trip down the lane for an 'airing'.

She was happier staying in bed and it was a battle to get her to walk a little and sit in a chair. Most things were a fight and she still wanted to go home.

By this time Jo had sold her house and she and Bill had moved into my mother's flat. I didn't blame her at all – it was such a lovely flat, and so convenient, but I couldn't bring myself to go there.

This way of life continued for about eighteen months and it was now Autumn 1990. Jo kept phoning, telling me I couldn't keep it up. I wasn't complaining – we were fine and I was well into the routine. It wasn't easy but she had been my mother and I wanted to look after her. Then Jo eventually told me she thought I was being selfish and hadn't I thought that my mother might be lonely and would prefer more constant company. She wanted her to go to a nursing home. I had promised my mother I would never do this and told Jo I didn't agree. I don't know why she was so insistent.

Was I being selfish? I wouldn't have thought so. True, she was left on her own for a couple of hours sometimes but she had more company than she did in the flat. She didn't know where 'home' was and she certainly didn't know Fairyhill. She knew me but I couldn't hold a conversation with her and she wasn't aware of anything that was going on. Perhaps it wouldn't make any difference where she was. I was gradually being worn down. John never persuaded me either way. I had looked after two aged aunts of his and helped nurse his mother for a short while so he would back me whatever I did, but I know he really agreed with Jo.

Maybe, deep down, I was relieved that the decision was being taken from me but I would never agree if I thought for a moment that my mother knew what was happening.

Well 'Strathmore' was decided upon after visits to a few other nursing homes and the arrangements made. This was only a quarter of a mile from where Jo lived so she could visit often. I tried to shut myself off. I would look after my mother forever as long as she was with me, but I didn't want to see her end up in a 'circle'.

Jo and Bill came to take her to 'Strathmore' and I looked from a window with the tears streaming down my face. I watched her climb into the car and her little suitcase go into the boot. They hadn't told her where they were taking her and I certainly hadn't. I don't suppose she would have understood what was happening – but I couldn't bear it. It was as they drove out of sight that I mentally buried my mother.

There were two sets of long low barns in the farmyard from which we could make four units. The builders started on the first one which we decided to call 'The Granary'. My plan consisted of a large kitchen/dining room with a stable door leading into the field. We would put a small patio out there eventually with table and chairs. There would be a sitting room and en suite bedroom which would look even more spacious with open ceilings and revealed rafters.

When the architect's plans came back to us for approval, John held them behind his back and said "Wait till you see what he's done to these." I was horrified to see that his drawings included a tiny hall and passageway leading to two minute bedrooms. Worse still were the glass doors and large windows. Why are architects obsessed with letting in as much light as possible regardless of the fact that big windows ruin the look and character of an old building? Once again, we had to insist that our original design be followed with the windows remaining the same size as originally built and a wooden stable door to let light in.

Why were we having to fight everyone? This determination to 'stick to ones guns' only comes with maturity. I used to think that the experts knew best and their advice had to be followed come what may. Unfortunately, experience shows that it pays to question certain things otherwise it would be easy to be landed with something definitely not wanted.

Although John agreed with me, he was very loath to tackle the problems with the builders and architects and pushed me forward to do the 'nasties'. On the other hand, he always dealt with officials, be they Public Health, Building Inspectors and particularly, anyone from the Planning Department – they were like a red rag to a bull to me!

Inside Granary

My theory on Planning Officers is that they have to say 'No' to a certain amount of things on principle. If we were ever to do anything else that required Planning Permission, I would ask for half a dozen things on the plan that I didn't need so that when they were refused everyone would be happy.

Once we were underway with the Granary, I could see that the entrance archway was not going to work. If we built a high wall across from the Barn to the Granary, it would stop all the late afternoon and evening sun from shining up the whole of the farmyard. We decided to compromise with a small five foot high wall and gate instead. The courtyard in front of this gate was crazy paved which looked nice but seemed to take forever to lay. We had ordered some wonderful Portuguese granite cobble sets to form a driveway all the way from the road to the top of the farmyard, a distance of about seventy-five yards which took fifty-five tons of granite. The pink hue of the granite blended in beautifully with the Gower stone of the buildings and that would make the astronomical cost well worth while. This is what we told ourselves when writing out the cheque!

Now that my mother was in Strathmore, I wasn't dashing around like a scalded cat quite so much.

I felt I had betrayed her and couldn't bring myself to visit but relied on Jo to tell me how she was. She appeared to be the only inmate not on medication, and chatted to everyone who came near her. She seemed to settle in alright and Jo even went so far as to say she was enjoying it. She had no idea where she was but at least, I suppose she had plenty of company. I couldn't bear the thought of her there and it would be a while before I could visit. It was all over to Jo now – I did what I could while she was in the outside world.

Chapter Twenty

Although John and I were still very fit, I was aware that he had lost a lot of weight. He got more tired than I did, but there again, he was ten years older, and men can't push themselves like women.

We occasionally had an evening out if the restaurant was quiet and we only had residents to feed. Lynne would be the one then to take the orders and generally look after everyone. Pat or one of the other girls would see to the bar and drinks and Lynne would concentrate on the food and wine. Lynne was so anxious to please that she sometimes got things wrong.

I overheard a conversation one evening, when a gentleman asked her if we did cocktails. To my amusement, I heard Lynne reply, "Do you mean, for instance, Penis Colada?" The man turned on his heels and I know he couldn't wait to get back to his group to relate that! It was ages before I could stop laughing enough to put her right. Needless to say, we have called them that ever since.

Apart from having the odd evening out, we were as busy as ever. I wanted John to have more rest but it was difficult. He would occasionally pop upstairs to watch the news at some time throughout the evening and, if at all possible, I would manage on my own for him to stay there. He could never totally relax and would imagine me struggling without him. I would have to promise to call him if I couldn't cope.

On one of our rare visits to a Swansea restaurant, we bumped into Kate and Clive. She had been in Chamonix for a year but was now back home looking for something else to manage.

I caught John's eye when she said this but we didn't say a word. I knew we were both thinking the same thing. If we didn't really want to sell Fairyhill who better to manage it? We could hand it over to Kate, live in the Stable and concentrate on looking after the grounds, knowing that everything would run smoothly. She knew how we liked everything done. What better solution could there be?

We talked it over on the way home. John had his doubts but I wanted to go ahead and ask her. The thought of being free, with time to ourselves was too tempting. We were victims of our own success now, and John needed a rest. He had enjoyed the challenge of Fairyhill; the struggle of getting it on the map and proving we could do it successfully when everyone had said it was impossible. It was an unrivalled triumph – loved by the local people and known all over the world. We had proved we could do it – now we could stop.

We decided to ask Kate if she was interested and, she was. I said, "You know how we like things run Kate, so we don't have to spell it out." After all, she had started Fairyhill with us.

She wanted a proper Contract of Employment drawn up with every stipulation itemised. All we wanted was for nothing to change without consulting us. This was all very legal and expensive involving accountants and solicitors.

Kate would start the second week of November. I would do the Christmas decorations but miss all the build up to Christmas. I wouldn't mind that at all! We had already decided not to open for Christmas Day so Kate would be eased in gently. New Year's Eve would be enough to start.

Now we had to move all our personal things over to the Stable. Kate would be moving into our room so everything had to go. Although the Stable was only about thirty yards from the house, it was quite a task and I made dozens of trips, my arms laden with clothes. I really must get rid of some – one day! They all came with me.

We were excited about everything and couldn't believe that now we would have the best of both worlds. We could concentrate on the grounds and everything we never had time for. The paths needed constant attention as did the front and back courtyards. The boundary walls had to be patched up and more land reclaimed at the bottom end of the orchard. The lake would soon need 'weeding' again and the weir needed repairs. These were the jobs that came to mind immediately and there would be plenty more. Cutting, collecting and splitting wood could take up one day a week.

The people who now lived next door to us in Stackpole Mill were also on spring water and their well was on our land, towards the north end. We had been meaning to do something about this for years and now that we had time to think, we took steps to give them this piece of land. We didn't charge them anything but they paid the legal costs. The land was important to them and we wouldn't miss it.

I was looking forward to my new life. I would find my spinning wheel and maybe go into production again. Perhaps try spinning dog hair and silk together. I had already combined dog hair and lurex very successfully. I could get my sewing machine out – I hadn't made any clothes for years! I could do a tapestry! This was wonderful – I had my life back. I couldn't understand how anyone could ever be bored.

Kate had been looking forward to taking over and was already making her presence felt. As we were completing our last moving out trip, I wished her luck. She thanked me and said, laughingly, "Don't forget, I don't want you two in and out over here."

We had no intention of interfering. We were only too glad to hand over. But on the other hand, we did intend to go for the occasional meal and perhaps enjoy the bar facilities now and again.

Anyway, we were far too excited with our new home to worry about that.

I shopped for groceries to stock the cupboards, bought polish and every day cleaning bits and pieces and generally wallowed in the pleasure of 'playing house'. I even enjoyed the novelty of hoovering. It was my own territory now and people would have to knock on the door before coming in. I could bath with the door open and walk around naked if I wanted to.

We still woke early but now didn't have to leap out of bed and rush around. We took it in turns to make the coffee to drink in bed. John would go up to the shop for his newspaper and luxuriously read it for as long as he liked. We didn't have to race the clock and it was wonderful. We hardly went out – just enjoyed the pleasure of being alone in our own home. We loved the Stable.

We were surprised to discover that Kate had no intention of sleeping at Fairyhill. She did stay over on the odd occasion when there was a late night but generally, she went home to Mumbles or stayed with Clive in Penmaen. What if someone was taken ill in the night, or needed something? What night number would they ring? We felt someone should be in residence.

A young waiter came over from France and he did live in. He slept in the 'wardrobe' – the large room above the pot wash and next to the Conference room. He wouldn't have been much use in an emergency as he didn't speak any English. I also wondered how he could communicate with the people he was serving.

True to our word, we didn't interfere and continued to enjoy our leisure. I made my first visit to the kitchen to wash a duvet in the big machines and had a huge welcome from the girls.

We booked a meal in the restaurant and looked forward to enjoying the pleasure of sitting in the dining room for our first totally uninterrupted meal. We had our drinks in the bar, ordered our meal and wine and ate our cockles, feeling very strange, just sitting there doing nothing! We were the second table to be called and when we arrived in the Billiard room the first couple were waiting for their starters. Our red wine hadn't yet arrived and we felt rather apprehensive.

I didn't enjoy myself. The food was excellent but there were long delays and not a very good atmosphere. Kate appeared very busy and everyone seemed ill at ease. Was it because we were there?

The menu had been expanded so that Jay and Julie found it hard to cope. They were working many more hours and getting home late. The staff had almost doubled and John was worried. These extra wages together with Kate's salary were way out of line.

We tried to tell ourselves that it didn't matter and we were bound to feel strange. We were out of it and we had to switch off.

Kate had been running Fairyhill for just six weeks and it was now Christmas. I was glad that we had decided not to open. Julie had said that she wasn't happy and had walked out on one occasion.

We had a miserable Christmas. I knew that we had to talk to Kate but didn't want to spoil her time off. Eventually, I telephoned her on Boxing Day. I told her I didn't think it was working out and things were not being done the way we wanted and we would have to call it a day. She said she had planned New Year's Eve and would like to do that before she finished but we decided against it.

We spent the time between Christmas and New Year carrying everything back from the Stable! Well, we'd had six weeks' holiday which we had enjoyed even though most of it had been spent worrying.

Kate came to collect her personal things a few days later and we parted amicably. She was off on a ski-ing holiday and we were back to work!

New Year's Eve had always been a set menu at a set price with many of the same people attending every year. This time there were a lot of new faces – maybe contacts of Kate's. It was soon apparent when they arrived that they hadn't been told that it was a set price menu and there was a lot of bad feeling. One table of nine were so unhappy that we invited them back for another evening as our guests. We had always explained the procedure to people when booking and asked if they would like a copy of the menu before confirming.

We got through the night but it wasn't the normal enjoyable relaxed evening of other years. We were glad when it was over.

We were now back at the helm and in a strange way it was quite a relief. We knew things had been going wrong and were glad to return. Kate had been keen and tried to smarten everything up and make it more French and professional. She didn't see that the way we ran it was part of its charm. If we'd wanted a trained professional who had been through the 'sausage machine' to run it – well, they were two a penny. We hadn't wanted Fairyhill brought into line. I had been sure she had understood that and it was quite a shock to realise that for all these years she was convinced we'd being doing it wrong. Anyway, it had been worth a try and we learn from experience. Although we were left respectively licking our wounds and nursing hurt pride, we parted without cross words and still remain good friends.

We decided that if we were continuing, we would make life easier. We cut out all conferences and most weddings. We didn't owe any money and were, in fact, doing very well so we didn't need to burst ourselves any more with overwork. We decided to close for the months of November and December every year. Marian could move in when we went away and we could enjoy some travelling and decent holidays. It would be lovely to lead a leisurely life for two months a year and take a deep breath. This seemed very sensible and although it was alien to John to refuse big bookings, he did agree that we should slow down and only do what we could enjoy. Now we could go on indefinitely.

On my last visit to the dentist, I had received quite a shock. I had apparently been under so much stress over the last few years that I had taken to grinding my teeth whilst asleep. I was totally unaware of this but was advised to wear some sort of gum shield to protect my teeth during the night. This was ridiculous. I had no idea I was in such a state of tension – it obviously was time we slowed down.

The only difficulty with closing for such a long time was the staff disruption. Jay and Julie quite liked the idea of extra time off as did a few of the others but some took jobs at various other places and we had to risk losing them. As it happened, they couldn't wait to come back to us. They didn't like working in the outside world!

I remember, years later, meeting Sally and Katie, the two young sisters who had been with us through school and college vacations. They had waitressed, cleaned and cooked. They told us that they had been very disillusioned when they took up permanent jobs. It wasn't at all like Fairyhill where everyone had mixed in and helped each other – home from home, and not like work at all. In fact, their parents had always said that working with us was better than an expensive finishing school. Their girls had learnt so much – and been paid.

Celyn and Winni were both fine but I could tell that little Annwyl our tortoise shell cat, wasn't well. She was off her food which, for a greedy pig like her must be serious. We did all the usual things such as worming. Our cats ate most of what they caught and had to be wormed regularly. She didn't want to cuddle anyone – usually she couldn't bear to see an empty lap! I tried feeding her with Complan and a dropper but she got thinner and thinner. I took her to Brookie who gave us some homeopathic pills but she didn't hold out much hope. I eventually took her to the Vet who also thought it hopeless. I wasn't going to give up and wanted a second opinion. I went to Brookie's vet who unfortunately confirmed that there was nothing to be done. They thought that what she had suffered as an abandoned kitten had done the damage and she had been on borrowed time. Poor little Annwyl. I had to leave her at the Vets to be put to sleep. I couldn't stay while they did it – I wasn't prepared and cried all the way home. I don't know how I drove safely. She might have had a miserable time as a stray kitten but she had a lot of love and affection from everyone in the three years she was at Fairyhill. Everyone missed her – except Winni-the-Purr, who had always hated her!

Chapter Twenty-One

We had another booking from Decca. They had been a few times since 'Adriana Lecouvrer' with various smaller productions. Richard Bonynge stayed on three further occasions and had fallen in love with the Stable. He loved the quietness and space and said he had the best nights' sleep apart from at home in Switzerland. He phoned his wife and told her all about it and she sent her love to us – How nice!

I remember on one visit, he wasn't well. He had a cold and an upset tummy from travelling. He was sitting in the bar with Andrew, the Producer and said he wasn't going to eat but would go to bed. John mixed him a port and brandy and practically forced him to sip it, promising he would be cured. Andrew was making faces and shaking his head and R.B. was sceptical. Anyway, Andrew ordered his meal and by the time it was ready, the magic had worked. They both went into the dining room and we had another satisfied customer!

Vladimir Ashkenazy had also made some more visits, on one occasion, bringing his wife. I always thought this the ultimate compliment, when people returned with wives or husbands.

He was such a nice man – so kind and friendly. It never ceased to amaze me that the big stars who stood in front of vast audiences, accepting the adulation of millions, could be so ordinary and unassuming. I always got a kick out of it.

The Decca visit was for 'Gloriana' by Benjamin Britten, with quite a large cast. We had with us Josephine Barstow, Philip Langridge, Alan Opie, Janice Watson, Yvonne Kenny and John Shirley-Quirk. These were as many as we could accommodate in addition to the engineers and production team. The engineers and Andrew and Jane were now like old friends visiting and everyone was at ease. They always said it made their job so much more pleasurable knowing they would be coming home to happy evenings.

Sir Charles MacKerras was conducting Gloriana. He and other members of the WNO had been to eat with us on many occasions and were always invited to the various end of recording parties. He was an Australian and we liked him very much. Carlo Rizzi had recently taken over the musical directorship of the WNO and we met him soon after he arrived. I enjoyed so much entering in to this glamorous world.

Not long after this Decca visit, we were very thrilled to have a booking from Dame Kiri Te Kanawa. She was also recording in the Brangwyn Hall, I think, with EMI and had heard of us from some opera friends. This recording was being sponsored by Peter Moores who was also staying with us.

Dame Kiri had asked for the Stable and duly arrived. The first thing she wanted was a 'nice cup of Welsh tea' and the three of us enjoyed this, sitting in the garden. She was a delight and very down to earth.

As Peter Moores was the only other member of the party staying with us, I asked her if she would be wanting to eat with him. She said she didn't like getting involved with sponsors and would we mind not telling him that she was staying here. Well, this was awkward.

She loved the Stable and asked if she could have her evening meals brought over. This would keep them apart for the evenings, but there was still breakfast. How would we stop them meeting? As luck would have it, Dame Kiri was always over by eight o'clock whereas Mr. Moores never breakfasted before nine. It worked like a charm.

Kiri was on a diet and I promised I would be very careful what I brought her to eat. She left the choice to me and I worked it out with Jay and Julie. We were most conscientious. They made everything very appetizing and attractive while I worked out the calories. She was most appreciative but fell by the wayside after discovering our Bread and Butter pudding – she was hooked on it and even took the recipe home with her.

They were with us for ten days, but when Mr. Moores had booked initially we could only accommodate him for a week, as we had a previous reservation for his room for one night only. He said he would move into the 'Marriott' where the rest of the cast were staying but would then continue the rest of his visit with them as it would be too much trouble to come back to us. This made sense and we quite understood. However, after his one night stay at the Marriott, he telephoned me early the next morning. I remember, I had just started cooking breakfasts. "Is my room still available Midge – I want to come back please?"

While he was at the Marriott, he of course, discovered that Dame Kiri wasn't staying there. He couldn't believe she had been at Fairyhill all the time. When he tackled me about it and asked why I hadn't told him, I said "Good heavens, Mr. Moores, don't tell me you didn't know that – I naturally assumed that you had seen her." They say that the best form of defence is attack!

Towards the end of this visit there was to be a dinner for the whole team including WNO high ups. Dame Kiri wanted to host a pre-dinner reception with champagne and canapés. She asked if she could have it 'in my little house' and it was a big success. The weather that evening was glorious and people spilled out onto the patio and lawn from the kitchen and sun room. I didn't do her canapés as requested but served our deep fried cockles which were far more of a novelty. Everyone loved her little house and explored every inch – various artistes singing from the gallery! I had great difficulty in persuading them all over to the dining room for their meal. At least now, after all these years, I had learnt that I had to start moving a 'laid back' party of people ten minutes before I really needed to. It was a wonderful night.

There had always been a lot of enquiries for lunches but we didn't want to get involved with split shifts for the kitchen staff. Jay and Julie travelled quite a long way and it would be impractical for them to get home in the middle of the day. We wouldn't be guaranteed a sufficient number of people wanting lunch to warrant keeping on highly-paid staff.

I can't remember exactly how it came about, but we began to do bar lunches. They were quite different from the evening meals – food that didn't need too much skill to prepare – food that I could do!

There was always soup, which just meant making extra for the evening. I pre-cooked rice and spaghetti and made bolognese sauce, curry, ratatouille and garlic mushrooms to accompany. Also Chilli con carne. In addition, there were various salads or a plate of smoked salmon.

John and Midge in kitchen

We had Nancy Morgan's granary french sticks which were quartered and crisped in the oven with every order. These were particularly popular filled with grilled bacon. A plain 'ploughman's' was wonderful with crisp bread, room temperature cheese and homemade pickle and onions. John and I had always judged a pub on its 'ploughmans' and it's amazing how many places can't produce a decent bit of bread and cheese. Before now we have been presented with a plate full of polythene packets!

I also had available chicken breasts and salmon fillets both served with a sauce and boiled new potatoes. Our dessert menu was of course, available.

These bar lunches we only did through the summer and they proved to be very successful and got us a mention in the 'Good Food Guide'.

We managed with just me in the kitchen, John in the bar and Marian serving. It was an absolute riot and I guarantee that no other establishment was run like it.

I had everything more or less ready in the kitchen – all laid out ready to be grabbed. I could then go about my other jobs and wait for people to arrive. Sometimes no one came and other times we could have about forty!

The routine was that Celyn would hear a car and bark. Marian would rush to the window, count the people then find me on the internal telephone and said "car pulling up with three people." I would then switch on both ovens and the grill and generally panic into action. If a few cars arrived together, John would have to be found. He was usually mowing and within shouting and arm waving distance. He would come running to man the bar. Occasionally, it would be a false alarm, so everything would be switched off again and John return to the garden. This could be repeated several times on a bad day!

We had no way of knowing how busy we would be as, unlike the evenings, not many people booked in advance. If it got really busy, Vera and whoever else was cleaning would stay on to help Marian out front. It was a lot for her to serve, prepare desserts and coffee. I was like a whirling dervish in the kitchen trying to do everything on my own. I was highly organised and had all ingredients to hand and there were no delays. The only time I got in a mess was when my friend Stephanie called in the middle of service and wanted to help. It took me too long to explain things to her and I completely lost my rhythm. I had to tell her to go away!

On busy days it was a very hectic two hours and my adrenalin level would be on overflow. By the time the chefs came in at half past two the kitchen looked as though a bomb had dropped. They were very good and cleaned it all up for me. I often did twice as many covers lunchtime as we did in the evening.

People would not only eat in the bar but also the garden, dining room and conservatory. On hot days, tables would be carried down the lawn and put under the trees. Could there be a more idyllic place for lunch? Wonderful for everyone but hard work for Marian's little legs!

We would have to get an extra potwasher in the evening to cope with the lunch dishes, or else, if we had a quiet night a single pot washer would come in an hour earlier.

We had a super nucleus of young lads washing up. All about seventeen or eighteen years of age and very efficient and sensible. Phillip, Geraint, Richard and Nolan. Clean living and adult in their outlook yet full of fun. They also did their own rota and would pitch in and help anywhere. They enjoyed a chat with the girls and didn't like to miss out on anything! John always quoted them as an example of the younger generation. He said they restored his faith. People are quick enough to knock them but our boys were great.

As well as washing up, they were very keen to have a try at 'waitressing' as they called it. We were pleased at their enthusiasm and they took it in turns to be trained and have an evening in the restaurant. They were a big hit, all spruced up, complete with bow ties – so different from the soggy tramps in the potwash.

We had a visit from the touring Australian rugby team during their trip to Wales. The whole party had booked in for Sunday lunch – about forty in all, and they really made themselves at home. They had had a gruelling week and were very tired. A few of them had a sleep before lunch and were to be found in various quiet corners – one desperate individual even on the drawing room floor. They had enormous appetites which I suppose, is not surprising for such huge young men. I saw that we prepared double the amount of potatoes, which proved to be a wise move.

We didn't do too well on the bar as they had brought a vast amount of XXXX beers in one of two iced containers on wheels, with Coca Cola in the other. They all drank from the cans so that saved on glasses.

They ate in the Billiard room and kindly signed lots of autographs. Richard and Phillip, who both play rugby, were washing up and at the end of the meal Lynne took them both in to meet the players. They were quite overwhelmed and were made a fuss of. They spent a good half hour chatting to the coach and were oblivious of the mounting pile of dishes!

It was now 1992 and we had long since finished the Granary which had turned out as attractive as the other three cottages. A lot smaller but still spacious with a cosy feel. We hadn't put a woodstove in this one as it meant explaining to people how to use it and also supplying wood. The stoves are really a way of life and people have to get to know their characters and quirks! We still had a very attractive fireplace there as a focal point but with, I'm afraid, a coal effect electric fire. We had not started on the Granary's next door neighbour, which was to be called 'The Dairy'. We had decided to wait a while and Derek had moved on to another job.

The Coach House, Stable, Barn and Granary had proved a big success and were now often used for self-catering holidays. People visiting Fairyhill would see them and sometimes stay there with their families. When not booked for holidays we could, of course, continue using them as extra rooms or suites, so we had the best of both worlds. Even our self caterers would often come across to the hotel for lunch and dinner and sometimes, even breakfast.

In addition to the still derelict Dairy, there were another group of outbuildings, the same size as the Granary and Dairy for which we had Planning Permission but had decided to re-roof these and leave them for storage. We would instead, convert two other barns into one larger house. I did the plans for this but we had no immediate urgency to proceed. We would have to accumulate some more money first. Rebuilding in stone was the only way we would contemplate the renovations, but it practically doubled the cost of labour.

We never liked cutting corners and used only the best in the way of materials. These buildings would hopefully, still be here in another few hundred years and they would be our legacy to the future. Rather a romantic outlook perhaps, but it was a thought that pleased us.

It was John's sixty-fifth birthday in November 1992 and I decided to give him a surprise party. We were closed so everyone would be able to come. It was mostly just staff with their husbands, although quite a few friends also found their way. I had arranged for our group of the Pontardulais boys to come and we had a really wonderful time. They were on top form and everyone let their hair down. John was thrilled and delighted to see his 'boys' again. It went on into the early hours as no one wanted it to end!

Our young friend Dominic, who had spent that first summer doing all sorts of work at Fairyhill, came to visit. He always talked fondly of those days and said it had changed his life. He would have loved to go into the hotel business. Instead, he had joined a bank and had a bright future. He had such a wonderful personality and both John and I thought he would have been superb in this business. One thing led to another and before we knew it, he was talking about buying Fairyhill from us. He was deadly serious and very excited. He took the books and made enquiries about finance.

What a whirlwind. We hadn't had time to think but we would have been pleased to pass our baby over to Dobs. Fairyhill would be going to a sympathetic owner who loved it as we did and we could help out if and when required.

Dobs had recently become engaged and his next visit was with his fiancé. It soon became apparent that Linda was interested but more intent on starting a family as soon as possible. This put a different light on the situation as far as John and I were concerned. It was a hard enough life if both members of the partnership were keen but a recipe for disaster in Dobs' situation. We had a very honest discussion and eventually, he agreed that we were talking sense. What a shame!

John and I seemed to be forever carrying various tables from one room to another. For certain functions one of the refectory tables was brought from the conservatory to the billiard room in exchange for the smaller Pembroke tables. There was plenty of juggling around depending upon whether there were more 'twos' or larger parties. It happened so often that it became a joke between us and we giggled our way up and down the corridors and argued who was to go backwards!

We had two large tables with folding legs that Pat Roach had made for us. They were enormously heavy with metal legs. These were only used in emergencies and were kept in the staff room, leaning against the wall.

One Sunday morning, I moved these and must have failed to stand one of them up properly. I turned to do something else when the table fell over and I caught the full weight of it down my ankle and onto my foot. I couldn't breath with the pain or even call out but luckily, Jay had seen it happen. She came with one bowl of hot water and one of cold and proceeded to bathe my foot alternately from each. She was making soothing sounds and saying "Go on, cry Midge, cry" as I still fought for my breath. I don't think I have ever been in so much pain – and my threshold is apparently high!

I eventually managed to get myself upstairs and plastered a large pad of lint with arnica ointment and bandaged my foot. I lay on the bed and eventually cried, feeling very sorry for myself.

As I said, it was Sunday and luckily, I had finished all the preparations for lunch. Everything was ready and all I had to do was change. It never occurred to me that I wasn't well enough to work! John had no idea what had happened – he was busy preparing the bar but he did eventually come looking for me. I took a couple of aspirins and rested for half an hour. I managed to get on a comfortable pair of shoes. They had a one and a half inch heel which was easier than being totally flat.

I got through the next four hours quite well but by the end of the afternoon my foot was extremely swollen and I was forced to rest.

I had broken a bone in my foot and it was ten weeks before the last of the technicolour bruising disappeared. I kept going all the time thanks mainly, I think to willpower, Jay's quick treatment and the arnica ointment and pills.

As we had never had a salvage collection, we had been in the habit of burning all cardboard boxes and any other rubbish, in the big walled garden at the back of the staff patio. We always kept an eye on any fires and they were never left unattended. The site of the bonfire was, I suppose, in the same area as the woodshed, but the opposite side of the path and not close enough for any anxiety.

John had bought a brand new machine for cutting the grass – a large Kubota diesel, and he was delighted. He had only used it once and had put it under cover – in the woodshed. This wasn't really a shed but a large open sided corner area of the garden with a roof supported by pillars.

He had left the bonfire, which was almost out, and gone to the bottom of the garden. He said that on looking back he had seen a lot of smoke – but from the wrong side of the path – not the bonfire! He ran back to see his lovely new machine alight! "Quick, somebody – fire." I don't know where I was but Diane was on her own in the kitchen and came running out with a hosepipe which she pointed at the tyre that was alight. The woodshavings on the floor had ignited and were glowing well. Diane was hopping from foot to foot on the hot floor waiting for the water to shoot through the end of her hose. In the meantime, John appeared with buckets of water. He had removed Diane's hose to fill his buckets. What a hoot – I don't know why no one had thought of the fire extinguishers! Anyway, the fire was put out with only the burnt tyre, blistering paint and very sheepish looks!

Chapter Twenty-Two

During the six years that Jay and Julie had been with us they had both married. Jay had been 'broody' from an early age, but Julie had never shown much interest in babies. However, Jay must have infused her with enthusiasm and now both were pregnant within two months of each other – how very inconsiderate!

We had to make plans and decide what we were going to do. This was a major upheaval with both of them leaving and I couldn't face the search for two new chefs. Perhaps we could close altogether and just enjoy living here. Even better, do bed and breakfast through the summer as we had originally planned – yes.

As we were now closing during November and December, Jay decided it wasn't worth her starting back. She was never totally healthy and enjoyed being at home. Julie was the opposite and determined just to have her ten weeks maternity leave before coming straight back to work. Once Jay had finished it meant that Julie had more to do. Diane was wonderful but wouldn't take the responsibility of main courses for some reason. She was too afraid of making a mistake. Melloney took over Sunday lunches which was good. Diane was usually in with her and the third person would be either Sally, Katie or Richard, who was Marian's son. Phillip from the pot wash was extremely interested and would also work in the kitchen as often as possible.

We had to get through the ten weeks that Julie would be off work and there seemed nothing for it but to advertise for help.

This was now 1993 and fate once more played its hand when we met Kate, who was back in Swansea looking for some summer work. She was terrific in the kitchen which was where we wanted her. It would be an easy way out and save all the worry and hassle of interviewing. If we were closing through the winter it would be difficult to employ someone short term. It suited Kate to fill in for that short time, so we agreed. She would start when Julie left to have her baby.

Soon after all this was agreed, we had an offer from some people who were interested in buying Fairyhill. Now, what were we going to do? The market was depressed and it wasn't a good time to sell, but on the other hand, did we want to be free? Even closing through the winter, it wasn't really the type of property that could be left empty for any length of time. We would have to pay someone to man the telephone and if that person lived in, there was the enormous cost of heating the whole house. We were very undecided.

We knew two of the people concerned. Paul and Andrew ran a very successful wine bar in Mumbles. They intended a partnership with Andrew's sister Jane, and her husband, Peter.

It was tempting and maybe if we waited until we were ready to sell, we wouldn't be able to find a buyer. Nothing had happened the first time we had put it on the market. I was quite happy to carry on but John, I know, was desperate to travel and also wanted to get back to his golf. He had wanted to see the world since he was a little boy but never had the time. He was older than I was and I mustn't be selfish. I could be happy doing anything but there were times when he got very tired. I suppose the decision made itself once I'd thought things through.

Now we had a second offer from friends who loved Fairyhill and just wanted to live in it. Was this confirmation that we were right to sell? I believe that fate shows the way – it's up to us if we take notice.

We agreed with Paul and Andrew that they would take over on 1st October 1993 which meant we had the summer at Fairyhill – time to say goodbye properly.

Julie finished just before Easter so Kate was straight in at the deep end. Easter was by far the busiest weekend of the year and she had her work cut out to cope. Every room was taken including the four cottages, and the restaurant was full Friday, Saturday and Sunday nights. Of course, Easter Sunday lunch was always a sell out for weeks before and there would be a waiting list for cancellations. Bank Holiday Monday went quieter in the hotel and restaurant as most people travelled home, but I was always kept busy with bar lunches.

The word soon travelled round that we were selling and people seemed genuinely sorry. What were they going to do? It wouldn't be the same. How could we do it? We said we were sure it was going to continue in the same vein and wouldn't be commercialised at all. The staff were naturally upset as they didn't quite know what would happen to their jobs. Well, it was five months away and we had the summer to get through.

Kate had only been with us a month when she had a week's holiday. She had also told us previously that she had made plans for two weeks in July. We thought Julie would be back then but she decided not to return.

There was nothing for it but for me to fill in. I had always dreaded this happening but it would only be for Kate's weekly night's off and her two holidays. She would take me through it all and keep the menus simple. I suppose I could manage it for a short while. This meant I would be doing breakfasts, lunches and occasionally dinners!

The first week I had in the kitchen, we had James Mallinson, an opera recording producer staying with us. He had been several times over the years and been to many dinners with us. He was desperate to arrange a big dinner at Fairyhill for all the cast. He asked me the day before he wanted it held and I was so upset. I had to refuse on the grounds that I just wasn't confident or capable of doing it. There would be about thirty people and there was no way I could cope with that number all at once plus all the residents. I really felt I and Fairyhill had let him down. It was my first experience in the kitchen for any length of time and I knew my limitations. I thought it better to refuse than risk tarnishing the reputation of nine years.

I got through the first week, but what would happen in July? That was our peak time for holiday people. Cross the bridge when we come to it and take things day by day.

We had agreed to sell the Coach House with the hotel and grounds but would retain the Stable, Bothey House, two smaller walled gardens and the small building at the entrance to the orchard. We would be moving into the Stable and this time there were even more things to carry across.

We were undecided about the farm buildings. Whether to sell the whole farmyard, or even sell off the houses as individual homes. It was too soon to come to any conclusions. We would let the dust settle. In the meantime, we decided to proceed with the renovation of the Dairy.

This time we employed Brian Ace, a local builder who had seen and admired the barns that Derek had done and knew the standard

Barns before new roofs

Same view

we required. I did warn him that I had very definite ideas and would be on his tail, but he seemed quite confident about working with me!

The summer was progressing with Kate's second holiday looming up. I was extremely anxious and decided I would have to limit the numbers of non-resident diners. She did do a lot of preparation for me with vast notes but, nevertheless, it was a big responsibility specially at this busy time. I was no chef. Yes, I could cook for my own dinner parties, but this was a totally different ball game.

Well, the time came and went and I managed it. I felt as though I never left the kitchen from morning till night, which was more or less true but I got through it without any disasters and no one seemed to notice any difference. I even had quite a few compliments! John had been concerned for me but I don't think he realised exactly how much I suffered. Every time he saw me looking anxious, there came the encouraging phrase, "You can do it, Babe." Well, Babe had now covered every job. Cleaner to chef and gardener to handyman, and every challenge thrown at me had been met. It was quite gratifying. I remember Jay saying once, "I'll say this for you Midge, – you'll have a go!" It was only my determination that carried me through.

Kate was back and I had time to concentrate on the hotel once again. We would be taking all our personal furniture and bits and pieces that we had always had in our homes, but would leave everything else. The new owners would need all the help they could get; starting, I presumed, as we did with a big loan. Anyway, they were taking over a thriving business. The hard work of getting Fairyhill on the map had all been done and it was now well known with a wonderful reputation. All they had to do was continue in the same vein and they couldn't go wrong. There were four of them so they could share the load and not work the long hours that we had. At least it would continue as a private family business with a personal feel, and wouldn't end up full of fruit machines!

The summer continued and we were gradually telling all our regulars of the new owners. With luck, we would be able to bid farewell to them all during the few remaining months.

Unfortunately, this was not to be. Instead of enjoying what time we had left, I couldn't wait for the end to come.

Kate had made an appointment to have a small operation on her knee. She was such an athlete and I wondered what on earth could be wrong. She seemed to run or cycle everywhere. She said the knee bothered her after she had run five miles. I thought there was an easy solution to that! This was a minor operation which would be over and done with in twenty-four hours and she would only need a day off.

After the day in question, Clive phoned to say she would need another day as something wasn't quite right. It transpired that she had developed thrombosis and had to be off work indefinitely. She never did come back, except on a pair of crutches to collect her things!

I couldn't believe that this was happening. It was the end of July and we had August and September to get through. If we'd had a crystal ball, we could have completed the sale earlier.

I musn't panic. I'd taken over the kitchen before and if I had to do it again, I would. The difference now was that I was on my own. I phoned Julie and asked her to help but she wasn't able to. I felt totally deserted.

Now I would have to prepare menus, see to all the ordering of fish, meat, vegetables and everything else before getting to work in the kitchen. I would have to make certain there was always plenty of stock available for the sauces. The stock would be left on the stove overnight on a very low light but I made many journeys down to the kitchen through the nights to check that it wasn't boiling over or that it was simmering at the right level!

In addition to the kitchen, there was still the restaurant to organise, tables, flowers, laundry – and builders.

I would have to keep the menu simple and cut the choice down to four starters and four main courses. It was our busiest time but we would have to control the numbers. Our poor non-residents would be the ones to suffer – and we had been hoping to spoil them all during these last months. What a shame, we were so looking forward to an enjoyable 'easing out' period and now I would be totally tied to the kitchen, morning, noon and night. John was confident that Babe could do it. Had he married me for my potential?

John was not only running the bar, but also taking the orders – a job that I had always done. Lynne was liaising between me in the kitchen and John in the bar so that he knew what I had available as the evening progressed. If Lynne was delayed and left him stuck in the bar, he would telephone through to the kitchen with a query which meant me leaving the stove to answer the phone and losing my concentration. It wasn't unknown for him to take an order for something which had run out, and things got very fraught. Lynne usually managed to make us all see the funny side and we survived.

All the girls were wonderful. I had Diane with me most of the time in the kitchen. I could manage up to eight on my own, starters and main courses, but anything above that and she would always come in. She was a gem for those two months. She hardly had a night off and really supported me through it all. Although it was mostly residents, we did do up to thirty-five some nights which, for just two of us was really hard work.

I definitely was not professional and needed four clockwork timers to help me remember what was ready in the oven. Every order I put in to cook would be timed and as long as I kept them in their correct rotation in the oven and respective timers in their place on the shelf, I was alright. This might have been unorthodox but it meant I never got mixed up or over-cooked anything. Impossible without my trusty 'pingers'. They went off constantly and only I understood what was happening!

The waitresses watched and encouraged me and instantly noticed if I missed a garnish or forgot something. It was all of us working through it together and although I was totally exhausted by the end of the night there was a euphoric sense of achievement. John always wanted me to come out front to chat, but some nights I was just too smelly and tired to bother. I did develop the habit of opening a bottle of champagne most evenings for Diane and me and everyone had a slurp. We deserved it and it brought our nerves back into line!

Towards the end of September we had a week's booking from BBC Television who were filming the Gary Rhodes cookery programme. They wanted the use of a kitchen and were delighted with the one in the Barn, which was huge. They were filming most evenings or visiting different places and I was very glad that they wouldn't be eating with us. My relief was short lived, as one night they booked a table for nine. I was dreading having to cook for such a famous chef but by now I had gained a little more confidence from all the compliments I had been having. Indeed, I needn't have worried. He was very kind and made a point of telling me how much he had enjoyed his meal. It was a thrill and put me on a high for quite a while.

The only time I had away from the kitchen in those last months was Sunday lunchtime, when Melloney took over. It was nice to be out front again and I felt that I had been set free into the outside world.

Although we had the TV crew as residents right up to the last, we decided to close the restaurant for the last three days of the month. I

cooked them breakfast of course, then they were out all day or filming in the Barn.

We needed this time for packing, moving and stock-taking the
wine and provisions. Although I was relieved that I had been freed
from the kitchen, I felt let down that I had missed what should have
been an enjoyable few months. Saying goodbye to regulars and having
the pleasure of giving complimentary drinks to all our faithful patrons.
There hadn't even been a proper farewell for the staff. I hadn't been
able to organise anything beyond the next meal! It was all too late
now and best forgotten.

Chapter Twenty-Three

When October 1st arrived the new owners seemed to be 'in' before I had even finished cooking breakfasts and certainly before the legal completion had taken place and I felt an intruder. There were strangers wandering around everywhere. Let's get the hell out and reach the sanctuary of our lovely Stable.

Kate had, by this time, fully recovered and had been asked to stay on by Paul. He would be head chef and she would take orders from him. Diane had been persuaded to help out a couple of days a week, which she did for a short time and Vera would also stay on as house-keeper. Apart from that everyone else was surplus to requirements.

We soon settled into the Stable as before but now we knew there was no fear of going back. Although we were so close to the main house, no windows overlooked it so we weren't aware of what was happening (unless we climbed up on to a high window-sill and really craned our necks!)

It was naturally very strange to be so close and yet have nothing to do with the running of things. It was like handing our baby over for adoption. It was hard also, to see many of our things we had left to help them, being thrown out with the rubbish.

We did, of course, make ourselves available in case any help or advice was needed, but this was never required. Naturally enough, I suppose. Our reign had ended and Fairyhill would never be quite the same again.

We decided that when the Dairy was finished we would get on with the last buildings. This would be called 'The Forge' and would be quite big and spacious. It consisted of a pig sty and two parallel barns which would be joined together with an additional room. As much as we loved the Stable, it would be better for us to move over there and be further away. We were too close to the hotel and it was

The Forge

Forge – second barn with "joining up" bedroom

hard not to count the cars, of both customers and staff. We were already concerned that there were too few of the first and too many of the second. Well, it wasn't our worry any more, but oh dear, it was hard to let go!

We were looking forward to having many meals at Fairyhill. It was so close and we could even pop over to have lunch in the garden sometimes. I think we should have waited a few months before going there. We went too soon and it was all too much of an emotional shock. Nice, but totally different. Very formal and quiet. No one spoke and everything was in the wrong place! The food was good but where was our lovely friendly atmosphere? Smiling waitresses had been replaced by silent uniformed waiters. Everybody has their own ideas I suppose, and we all think we're right.

The end of an era, and it took us a long time to unwind. We were revelling in our free time and I had to keep pinching myself to realise I had no pressures. My time was completely my own, but we found it hard to settle. We had heaps of things to do with the builders and we could now organise some holidays, but we were missing the company. Not only the guests but mostly the staff. After all, we had almost been living in a commune for the last nine years. There had always been people around and it would take time to adjust to a 'normal' life again. Celyn found it strange and we had to stop her wandering over to the kitchen door. They were not as 'doggie' as us.

We finished the Forge, which was a big success. It was like a huge ranch house, all on one level. The kitchen was enormous – thirty-six square yards, full of arches and wood – my two favourite things. The sitting room was also gigantic and open to the roof, like all our houses. There was a small 'den' for John and an internal courtyard for me. At last I could enjoy lying in the sun again. For the last ten years I had relied on 'joking' instant tan from a bottle! There were also courtyards on two other sides of the house so at any time of day I could find a place in the sun. There were two very large bedrooms, each with its own bathroom and a small conservatory, French doors led onto the enclosed courtyard from our bedroom, the kitchen and conservatory so it was just like an extra 'outside' room. I dreaded leaving the Stable and never thought I could ever love another house as

Kitchen in Forge – my very own!

much. I was mistaken. The Forge is a dream come true – just like our life.

We travel during the winter and have guests in the four cottages throughout the summer. The same people return year after year. Many who used to stay in the hotel now prefer to self cater with us and it's always lovely to see them again. A few of the Decca crowd are still regulars and so we have the pleasure of plenty of company without the long hours of hard work. We have social visits from both ex staff and ex Fairyhill regulars so, after all, we were not denied the pleasure of entertaining them, even if it is a little late. Whenever we get together, we reminisce fondly, laugh a lot and relive the short but most earth-shattering part of our lives.

Had we renovated our last house or had we learnt our lesson – who knows?

Update

It took us almost two years to 'extricate' ourselves from hotel life and in fact, it is only the writing down of these events that has finally purged me!

My mother died a year after we sold Fairyhill, closely followed by my dear friend Diane, who had worked with us for so many years.

Kate opened her own restaurant in Mumbles which is extremely popular and successful. Her cooking goes from strength to strength and we eat there often.

Fairyhill continues successfully and has an excellent restaurant. The bedrooms have been upgraded and enlarged and people continue to enjoy its beautiful surroundings.